PARDON
SPANGLISH

One Man's Guide to Speaking the *Habla*
¡Porque Because!*

BY BILL SANTIAGO

QUIRK BOOKS
PHILADELPHIA

For Papi and Mami

Library of Congress Cataloging in Publication Number: 2008924738
ISBN: 978-1-59474-213-2
Printed in Canada
Typeset in Bembo, Coop Latin, and Trade Gothic

·Grateful acknowledgment is given for permission to reprint "I Will Survive" by Frederick J. Perren
and Dino Fekaris, © 1978 Universal-PolyGram Int. Publ., Inc./Perren-Vibes Music, Inc. All rights
administered by Universal-PolyGram Int. Publ., Inc./ASCAP. Used by Permission. All Rights
Reserved.

Cover designed by Doogie Horner
Interior designed by Jesse Flood
Edited by Mindy Brown
Cover photograph by Jimi Robinson

To contact the author
E-mail: bill@porquebecause.com
Web sites: www.billsantiago.com, www.porquebecause.com,
www.myspace.com/billsantiagocomedy

Distributed in North America by Chronicle Books
680 Second Street
San Francisco, CA   94107

10 9 8 7 6 5 4 3 2

Quirk Books
215 Church Street
Philadelphia, PA 19106
www.quirkbooks.com

LOS CONTENTS

INTRODUCTION

Somebody had to write this book. Why me? *¡Porque because!*

Let me begin with a confession. I am a lifelong perpetrator of Spanglish. And, *debo subrayar*, proud of it. *Más aún*, whenever I hear that effortless flow of the *habla*, blatantly *bounceando* between bilinguals, *de veras que* it warms the cockles of my *corazón*.

Además, as a standup comedian, I am especially thankful for Spanglish because it provides so much laughter for Latinos and the Latino-curious. *Jamás me pudiera haber imaginado* how explosive a word like *chancla* could be in a comedy club. *Pero, la primera vez que* I tried it, *todo el mundo* went nuts and I knew I was onto something.

Not surprisingly, I wanted *un mejor* understanding *del* Spanglish. *Pero nadie* could ever explain to me *cómo diablos funciona este* compulsive mixing *de idiomas*.

It's no easy trick to make Spanish and English fit together so perfectly. *Y siempre me preguntaba*, how do we incorrigible *hablantes del* Spanglish do it *tan* seamlessly *cada santa vez?*

¿Cómo es que el brain *y la lengua* can sychronize *de tal manera* to make it possible?* What are the *principios fundamentales* at work? And what the hell does *"cójelo con* take it easy" really mean?

My inquiring mind *quería saber. Pero* the answers, *no se encontraban* anywhere. *De veras*, I'm not kidding you. *Leí* everything I could get my hands on *sobre el tema*, and came up with a whole lot of *nada*.

Y déjame aclarar, not everything was written by idiots, either. Some of the *distinguidos autores* were *muy educados*. But it turns out anyone *con la palabra* "emeritus" *siguiéndole a su título* is generally clueless about Spanglish.

Sin falta, either the material I found was too clichéd and frivolous or painfully *académico*, and totally *careciendo de un sentido del humor*. All in all, *¡flojísimo!*

Por lo tanto, this book is groundbreaking, if only because of how hard some of the language *puristas* will hit the ground *del desmayo que sufrirán* after reading it.

Un All-American *Idioma*

Enemies of the *habla* would like to dismiss the whole phenomenon, *como nada más que una jerga degenerada*. But shrugging off Spanglish as slang is like referring to *una tormenta de relámpagos* as "a little static electricity." *De hecho*, it's the *lengua traviesa* of an inherently funny people, reflecting their two component heritages *bundeleados* into one.

And verily I say unto *ustedes*, Spanglish *es un* all-American *idioma*. That's right, *nacido aquí mismo* and exported every day *al resto de latinoamérica* and beyond. Frankly, *se merece* a little more respect. Not to mention, *una investigación* that actually tries to capture its dynamic essence *en toda su comiquísima gloria*.

I should have never opened my big mouth, though. *Porque*, guess *a quién le tocó el* challenge? Correctamundo! Yours truly, *a las órdenes para servirles. Pues cuando este libro alcance a ser el primer* bestseller *de lengua* Spanglish *rankeado por el periódico* the *New York Times*, *pues*, it will have all been totally worth it. *Es más*, you're all invited to the party.

Mientras tanto, I promise you, *cualquiera que sean* your Spanglish goals, this book will pay for itself by the time *que termines* the introduction. Sooner, *si quieres* skip the rest of it. *Las introducciones solo son* foreplay *literario* anyway, *por si no lo sabías*.

Your Spanglish Journey

I don't know how *habla*-savvy you are. *Quizás* you've never even heard of Spanglish before, or never thought about it much, or never realized how much of it was going on all around you *en un* day-to-day basis. Or maybe *ni siquiera te hayas dado cuenta de* how much *ya lo estabas* talking yourself!

Maybe you're already proficient *pero deseas* greater Spanglishicity.

El asunto es que whether you just want to learn what Spanglish is, shoot the breeze informally *cuando estés chilaxeando con tus* Spanglish peeps, or be the first Spanglish translator at *Las Naciones Unidas*, my mission is to empower your every step *por el camino de tu* Spanglish journey.

Claro, en cierto sentido, we're all on a Spanglish journey, *le guste o no a quién sea.* It's the future, *y no podemos quedarnos estoqueados* in the past. *Podríamos* pretend otherwise. *Pero, ¿para qué engañarnos?*

Ahora bien, tales declaraciones are surely going to rub *algunos* conservative *infelices* the wrong way.

Pues, Bring It On

La verdad es que I'm kind of looking forward to being disparaged and denounced as a *barbaridad* peddler *de dudosa seriedad* and *escasos conocimientos.* As a comedian I have nothing to lose. *Además, se me hace* hilarious *el hecho de que* Spanglish gets attacked *tanto por los* English fundamentalists *como por los extremistas del español.*

Personally, I think of Spanglish as very pro-Spanish. I wage it as an act of *resistencia* against the assimilate-or-else mentality *todavía bastante presente* in a land where Spanish is far from the official *idioma.*

In these times of immigrant-bashing and rising minute-*manismo*, when speaking any Spanish in public practically gets you on a terrorist watch list in this country, I consider Spanglish a very noble *desafío* to the not-so-Latino-friendly *elementos* out there.

Yet, *mientras tanto*, many Spanish purists regard Spanglish as societal form of Tourette's syndrome, *peligrosamente contagioso* and threatening *el castellano* with extinction. Boy, are they *paniqueados*. And they're crazed with the kind of righteous outrage *que suda a snobismo*. I mean, these self-proclaimed *guardianes de la ortodoxia* act is if they had Faberge *cojones* or something.

Pero anyway, so be it. *La controversia es buenísima para la venta de los libros.* However, in light of the inflammatory nature of this book, *quiero hacer un pedido al público*. Please refrain from sectarian violence.

En cambio, if anybody *se muere de la risa*, that's OK by me.

Otherwise, enjoy this book *en paz*. Share it with friends—hundreds and hundreds and hundreds of your friends, *quienes les encantaría recibirlo como un regalo* (*en* hardcopy).

This is my baby, and I hope *que en estas páginas* you find *todo lo que* you ever wanted to know *sobre el* Spanglish, *pero estabas* afraid to ask.

Deseo que esta labor de tanto empeño y esperanza sirva both as a resource and a companion, to remind you *constantemente* of the single most persuasive argument for unleashing the Spanglish speaker within. *La vida es demasiado corta* to be monolingual.

¡Porque because!

1

SHAKESPEARE AND CERVANTES

ON THE A TRAIN

"If Spanglish becomes our official language, I don't think American taxpayers should have to shoulder the burden."

—concerned monolingual patriot

Spanglish is the Reese's Peanut Butter Cup of languages: Two great languages *que van* great together. "Hey, you put Spanish in my English!" "*¡Y tú pusiste* English *en mi español!*"

Only what may appear as an accident is actually coming to pass just like Nostradamus, the best guesser ever, predicted: "As two tongues are better than one, so they shall be spoken as one. Also, J.Lo will have twins."

Shortly after Nostrasdamus died (unexpectedly), Miguel de Cervantes and William Shakespeare immediately got cracking and produced their respective masterpieces, *Man of La Mancha* and *Westside Story*, originally under less successful titles.

Not only was it a jackpot *para los apasionados de los* Broadway showtunes.

Sino que también, that kooky, quill-pushing pair of showoffs, *a través de tales obras*, supercharged their respective royal lingos, *para que hoy en día el* Spanglish *pudiera* enjoy a best-of-both *mundos* destiny.

¡Que Viva el Outsourcing!

Call it Spanglish, Inglesñol, Mexicali Esperanto, Bodega-bonics, Chipotle-chat, the Queen's Pocho, La Raza 2.0, Casteyanqui, Illegalese, or Spic-speak. The *habla*, by any other name, is spreading *como loco*.

It's an unbeatable combination. Twice the vocabulary and half the grammar!

As global flux and porous borders *reinan como nuestra* reality, Spanish and English *siguen* mutually *outsourceando* from each other's dictionaries and idiomatic playbooks.

Listen up. It's all around you *salpicando* the air with amazing sound *bitecitos*. I collect them. *En vez de estar* people watching, I'm much more interested *en cómo la gente está* using their langauge, adapting it, *de acuerdo a sus necesidades*. And the Spanglish chatter in the system these days, *según mis observaciones*, is off the charts.

I Spy

My methods *pueden ser un poco* sneaky. I may look *como si estuviera* absorbed in my "USA Today *en Español*." But if you are engaging in a Spanglish conversation anywhere within earshot, I've got you tuned in loud and clear.

Te estoy cachando in the act. If you see me scribbling *algo*, it's not because I'm composing *una cartita* to the editor. I'm writing down *lo que acabas de decir!* Or, *si tengo* my cheap little *grabadora conmigo*, I'll start recording *sin pedir permiso.*

After years of nonconsensual eavesdropping on family and friends, *ahora me paso* stalking Spanglish-speaking strangers in search of *nuevas muestras* of the *habla*. The best hunting ground for Spanglish at large is, *sin lugar a dudas*, public transportation. Buses are good. *Los* subways *son* better.

I can always count on the A Train in New York *para un tremendo* motherload *de* Spanglish *día y noche*. I'm usually riding express between Columbus Circle and Washington Heights (a.k.a. *Quisqueya* Heights or *Guachington* Heights or *El Pequeño Cibao*, because, *como bien se sabe*, Dominicans rule past 145th). I live up there *porque*, although I'm Puerto Rican myself, I can't afford to live in a traditional "Westside Story" *boricua*-hood of Manhattan anymore, like Hell's Kitchen, which is now more of a breakfast nook. *Pero* I digress.

My point is the dizzying *idioma*-mix underground, *mientras volamos a todo lo que da* through what I call the *"Oprima el Dos* Corridor," with the occasional *mariachi* serenade by the Mexicans muscling into the soundscape, reflects the whiplash-inducing *vaivén* between two parts of the city boasting entirely different psycho-linguistic default settings, English and *otra vaina*.

But this is no underground trend. You couldn't get away from it if you wanted to. It's blaring over speakers at stadiums. ("Join us for post-game *mojitos.*") And being whispered in elevators. (*"Ay, no me digas que vamos para el* basement.")

Overheard

Coast to coast, *desde el barrio* to *los* boonies, from the local mall *hasta* your city hall, from the border to the boardroom, from the classroom to the roomiest sections of first class, *desde la oficina de tu dentista* to anywhere *que la gente esté cotorreando* on their Bluetooths (or *cualquier tipo de* cell phone), Spanglish is driving a remarkable and irreversible colloquial climate change. *¿Crees que exagero?* Here's a teaser of random samplings *de lo que he escuchado* here and there, to give you an idea of what you're in for *en los capítulos siguientes.* Read them quickly *para poder gozar el* full jumbled effect. Imagine yourself *sentado en el* subway, *en un vagón* jam-packed *de gente.* Let one quote roll into the next, *como si estuvieras* tuning in and out of different gab sessions all around you. And, *les advierto,* hold on tight.

"Seriously, *me hicieron una brujería* or something."

"You missed a good party. *Había mucha gente.* It was like buzzing *cuando yo llegué.*"

"*Huele* a homeless."

"*Pero qué* freakin' *casualidad que* I ran into *mi* ex at the DMV."

"*Por fin le dije,* 'Just chill out.'"

"*Oye,* Mr. Fashion. *Ese tatuaje de* Scarface *va muy bien con tu camisa* wifebeater."

"I want one of them iPhones. *¿Cuánto te costó esa vaina?*"

"Got back last night. *Y estoy* totally *jetlagueada.*"

"*¡Coño qué* ripoff!"

"Holly's date never showed up. Can you believe it? *La dejó plantá.*"

"Excuse me, *pero ¿qué tú te crees? ¿Que* I was born yesterday?"

"What's all the *bochinche* about?"

"All in all, *chévere.*"

"*Estoy* PMSing *algo brutal.*"

"*¡Pero por Dios Santo!* Get a life."

Bueno, it makes your head spin, doesn't it? But pretty soon everybody's gonna be talking *así mismo.* And if you can't, *estarás* up a creek. Or, if you prefer, up *el creeko.*

Nostradamus may have been the only one who saw it coming, *pero* two of history's greatest *lenguas maternas* have breached the lingual levies, *señoras y señores,* and there's no turning *pa'trás.* One thing *es seguro.* Every time *que* I swipe *mi tarjeta* through *la* turnstile, *tengo un* feeling *de que* Cervantes and Shakespeare *están* coming along for *el* ride.

So *bienvenidos* aboard the A Train. We're traveling express into another dimension, a dimension *más allá de lo que es conocido por* monolingual man, a dimension whose boundaries are that of imagination and *cojones.* It's a dimension laced with *¡Azúcar!,* where new *palabra*-treats melt *en tu boca,* not *en tus manos.* It lies between the pit of man's *habla*-phobia, and the summit of his impossible Rosetta Stone *sueños.* It is the middle ground between English and Spanish, between Strunk and White and *Sábado Gigante.*

Estamos a punto de hacer el crossover into *El* Spanglish Zone.

TOP TEN BEST THINGS ABOUT BEING LATINO

1. MEETING SIBLINGS YOU NEVER KNEW ABOUT.

2. NO ONE'S EVER GOING TO CALL YOU WHITE TRASH.

3. DATING INTERRACIALLY WITHIN YOUR OWN RACE.

4. DANCING MERENGUE ON THE A TRAIN TO YOUR CELL PHONE RING TONE.

5. NEVER HAVING TO SAY, "OOPS, AM I TOO EARLY?"

6. GUARANTEED PART IN HIGH SCHOOL PRODUCTION OF "WESTSIDE STORY."

7. NOT BEING IN JAIL MAKES YOU AN INSTANT OVERACHIEVER.

8. SINGLE BED SLEEPS EIGHT.

9. GLOW-IN-THE-DARK CRUCIFIXES.

10. WHEN MAKING LOVE, *"AY PAPI"* JUST SOUNDS SO MUCH BETTER THAN "WHO'S YOUR DADDY?"

2

IS SPANGLISH
A LANGUAGE?

Mind over grammar
It's so wrong, I can't do it
***Yo hablo* Spanglish**
—Spanglish haiku

Before I get into it here, *debo advertir que* if you don't agree *conmigo*, go write your own book. *Y asegúrate de que* it's at least *un poquito* funny, *¿OK? Porque* otherwise, *estos libros suelen resultar un tantito* boring. Trust me, *yo sí sé*, because I've read them all.

Otra cosa. Don't try to get away with reducing Spanglish to just *un bonche de* crazy new bastard words, either. *Ya estoy harto de recibir* those half-baked glossaries, *que siempre mis* well-meaning *amigos me están forwardeando por* e-mail.

As if that's all there was to it! Sure, ludicrous Spanglish *disparates* are loads of fun at parties. *Pero* limiting the idea of Spanglish to a loopy lexicon *da la impresión de que* it's nothing more than a fringe novelty. *Lo cual me parece muy equivostaken.*

Why is it always the same old stupid examples? For instance: "*El rufo está leakeando.*" That is the single most cited example of Spanglish ever. As if *todos nosotros* Spanglish-*hablantes* spent all our time sitting around under our leaky *rufos.*

> "What's the matter, Bill, got the sniffles?"
>
> "Yeah, *es que* that damn *rufo* of mine is always *leakeando.*"
>
> "When it rains?"
>
> "No, just *cuando me pongo a hablar el* Spanglish."

Such lame *ejemplos* are unfortunate. *No hacen nada para dar un* true appreciation *de cómo* Spanglish speakers actually *se comunican.* Yet *los* fools and *los* haters are all too quick to sell out the *habla* as something less than a real *idioma. Pero ojalá que* my humble efforts *en estas páginas* will help remedy that situation.

The Million-Dollar *Pregunta*

So let's stop beating around the *arbusto.* Is Spanglish a language?

Yes, *por supuesto.* Spanglish is one of the most innovative languages of our time, second only *quizás* to Klingon. And it requires much less *maquillaje.*

Why wouldn't you consider it a language? Because it's made up of other languages? *Pero, si no hay ningún idioma natural que se haya creado desde* scratch. *Resultan siempre* from intimate contact *entre otros idiomas.* There's no such thing as immaculate vocabulary. Coinage is messy and carnal. *Y de hecho,* most words *nacen* out of wedlock.

What else are you going to call it? Wait, please don't say "code-switching." *Ese término flojo* makes me cringe. *¿Cómo que* code *ni qué* code? First of all, *cuando escucho la palabra* "code," I think of top-secret military messages, not Spanglish. *Suena medio* silly, like lingo from a bad submarine movie.

> "Commander, we've intercepted a highly encrypted transmission from the enemy, but we were able to de-scramble it with an English-Spanish dictionary."
>
> "Good code-switching, Lieutenant."
>
> *"Gracias,* sir."
>
> "Excuse me?"
>
> "I mean, thank you."
>
> *"De nada."*

As a descriptive term, code-switching, *como se dice* . . . sucks. *No se trata de* codes, *sino de idiomas* and everything they embody: culture, heritage, emotional frequencies, ways of thinking and feeling. *El switcheo* is actually between co-dependent realities. *Así que* code-switching is obviously code for: *Estos chingados académicos* have no idea *de lo que están* talking about.

Don't you dare call it a dialect, either. I mean, a dialect of what? English (*gringo*-lect)? Or Spanish (*vida-loca*-lect)?

Se puede hablar igual de fluently *tanto por hablantes que son* English dominant *como los que son* Spanish dominant. Research by the *Porque* Because Consulting Group suggests that as the *habla* becomes more standardized, *a través de* Dora the Explorer and other pioneers, *tales distinciones* will become blurred, *tarde o temprano,* to the point of irrelevance.

Slanglish?

What about slang? Dissing the *habla* as *un puro* slang is really *el colmo del descaro.* Say it to my face *y se va a formar un tremendo revolú!* Slang is a set of informal words and phrases, *perteneciente a un* subculture, incorporated into an existing language. Spanglish *es un fenómeno mucho más abarcador.* In fact, the word "Spanglish" can also be used as a slang term for the slang incorporated into the Spanish language. *Me están* following? *Si no,* come back *cuando* you can focus. *Porque este libro no se llama* "Spanglish for *Tontos," ¿OK?*

Certainly Spanglish is a great generator of slang, and slang appeal creates *un tremendo* exchange between its two input languages. The thing is *que una traducción literal* into another language, by definition, deslangifies the *slangueo.* Nothing gets lost in translation like foreign slang, *por lo tanto es* normal *adoptarlo* as is. *Entonces* maybe *lo modificamos* just *un chipito* so that it matches its new lexical surroundings.

Por ejemplo, lately *está de moda combinar la palabra* "chill," *que significa* "to relax" *en la jerga gringa,* together *con la misma palabra* "relax," *resultando en el* super americanismo *de* "chillax." *Bueno,* that baby's just begging to be Spanglishized into "*chilaxear.*" *Es más,* by the time you read this, I'll be done writing and *chilaxeando en una playa* someplace, *escuchando el mar* murmuring to me, "You deserve *un breakicito, papi.* Have another *piña colada* and *chilaxéate . . .*"

Did I Say That?

So if you've been calling it code-switching, or a dialect, or slang, *por favor,* cut it out. *A pesar de que todavía estamos* working out *los* kinks, Spanglish is, *de una vez por todas,* a language. Although many people who speak this language *ni siquiera saben* that they're doing it.

Una amiga mía en Bakersfield, California, swears *que* she doesn't speak Spanglish *supuestamente* because she never uses *palabras* like *parquear,* or *trocka,* or *rufo,* even though she can barely get through a sentence without constant *switcheo* between languages. *"¿Qué* what? Who me? *Déjate de bromas* because I would never speak Spanglish," she says. *La mujer está en* total denial. *Pero* it's understandable *que ella no quiera* face the truth, *porque* she's a Spanish teacher. *Y obviamente, no ha hecho su* homework.

But *la verdad es que* Spanglish works best *cuando* you have no idea that you're doing it. Because *entonces* it doesn't sound forced or contrived, *tú sabes. Siempre* it's in that unaware flow *que el* Spanglish *logra alcanzar su* greatest justification *como un idioma* all its own, operating as an unconscious *modalidad bilingüe* in which English and Spanish *se están utilizando precisamente* as if they were one and the same outlaw *lengua.*

If you become too self-aware that you're speaking Spanglish, sometimes *de repente* you can't do it anymore. It can be like flying in a dream. *Tan pronto* you realize *que estás* flying, *¡olvídate!,* you fall out of the sky. *Y, en definitiva,* the most seasoned Spanglishistas *hablan* on autopilot, switching back and forth *sin darse cuenta.*

Lexical Attraction

Spanglish happens spontaneously because English and Spanish are so naturally attracted to each other. *Tienen* chemistry. Trying to keep them from combining would be like trying to prevent hydrogen and oxygen from pairing up to give us *agua.* And honestly, *me cae muy bien la idea de que* my body is 80 percent Spanglish.

We are *lo que hablamos*. Indeed, what we speak formats our reality, *mientras a la misma vez* providing the means to articulate it. Which begs the question, *¿quiénes somos?* Some of the opinions are not very favorable.

We Spanglishistas are often depicted somewhat less than charitably as a bunch of degenerate *incultos* who are at best functionally bi-illiterate and resort to Spanglish *sólo porque* we don't know English or Spanish very well. *Bueno*, OK, *a veces* that's a little true. But that doesn't explain my father, *un hombre muy educado* who worked very hard to keep a non-leaky *rufo* over our heads.

Mi queridísimo papi era un abogado, who graduated from Brooklyn Law School, and he spoke, read, and wrote both Spanish and English perfectly, with native fluency, *y a un nivel muy profesional*. He had neither a Spanish accent when he spoke in English *ni un acento americano cuando hablaba español*. And he went back and forth between the two, *como le daba la gana* or not.

Spare Some Change?

Not only is Spanglish spoken across the socioeconomic spectrum by individuals of all educational levels, it doesn't even matter *de cual país* your people come from. All roads lead to Spanglish. *Ni siquiera importa si eres latino*. Gringos are very much on board with the *habla* too.

By the way, I want to give a shout out to all you *gringos* reading along here. I hope you're enjoying *el booko*.

Latinosapiens *acabaditos de llegar a los Estados Unidos* speak it as English-infused Spanish, and subsequent generations *tienden hacia* Spanish-infused English, as the pendulum of relative proficiencies swings naturally. *Los gringos* join in *de acuerdo a lo que aprendieron en la* high school or picked up in one of those "*más cerveza por favor*" phrasebooks. It's all *el mismo mambo.* We're all doing our part, *aportando nuestro granito de arena* to advance our cause. Keep in mind, this is just the beginning. *Tenemos* big plans for Spanglish (official language of the United States, world domination, etc.). You should come to the meetings. But suffice it to say that the evolution is well under way.

A lo largo de los siglos, languages all change *drásticamente.* Whatever language you speak today is really just *una etapa pasajera* in the evolution of that language. Your grandkids' grandkids' grandkids' *nietos* wouldn't understand a damn thing you were saying *si pudieras hablarles*, because the language *habría cambiado tanto* by then *que no se reconocería como tal.*

Seriously, if you pick up a book written in Old English, *pero es decir* really old, *como* like way *antes de los* Beatles, you won't recognize a word of it, except maybe "the." And the word "the" didn't even mean "the" back then. *Significaba* "hippopotamus." *Pues, y* unless you know that, understanding *un libro como* "Beowulf" *es un* nightmare.

¿Cómo Que Crutch?

Hopefully, by the time the Spanglish of today is regarded as Old Spanglish, *algunos de los más* nasty misconceptions about it will have been *debunkeados.* In the meantime, I'd like to take a whack at misconception *número uno.*

According to one of the more balanced columns regularly posted on www.idioma-de-idiotas.com, titled "*Podrido de Anglicismos*," Spanglish *resulta* from "*carencia de vocabulario*" and "*pereza mental*." In other words, *supuestamente usamos* Spanglish as a crutch to save our ass when we don't know a word, because we're too *perezosos* to actually learn how to say something correctly. Maybe *a veces*. But to assume that's always the case, *sería un* big mistake. *Es más*, many times *se da lo inverso*. Sometimes we perpetrate the *habla* because we know more than one way to say something *y podemos escoger la manera* that best suits our needs or expressive whims *en un momento dado!*

Let me give you a perfect example. See, in Spanglish you would have a choice between saying, "*el alma de un frijolito que se va al cielo*" or the shorter English version, "fart." You have to admit the Spanish option *es un poco más* tasteful. So the accusation that Spanglish is only resorted to by an underclass of people with limited vocabularies *es puro pedo*.

Each language *tiene sus* advantages. Spanglish allows us to mix and match them. All things being equal, we instinctually choose to say something in whatever language *comunica* the exact nuance intended. There's no such thing as truly equivalent translations between languages, only approximations. Not only that, *algunos conceptos* exist only in one language.

Por ejemplo, I always remember my father warning my mother not to do anything crazy. But he would say it in Spanish. "*No vayas a cometer una locura*," he would say, using the closest Spanish idiom. This, however, changes the meaning, as it would translate back into English as, "Don't go and commit a craziness." See, in Spanish you don't just do something crazy. You commit a craziness. Like a murder. We're very serious about our *locuras*. And we're always warning each other not to commit one. Although, in my mother's case, such warnings *casi siempre* backfired.

Pero anyway, it's not just about the words, *sino también el hecho de que hay diferentes aspectos conceptuales* at work in each language universe. You can't conceive of committing a *locura* in English, because the exact concept does not exist in that language. Don't even commit the *locura* of trying it. You may get caught and end up in jail for premeditated *locura*. And, *como quien dice*, if you can't do the time, *no vayas a cometer la locura*.

¿Y Qué, So What?

For me, the *locura* would be not switching back and forth. *Sería como un* mental straight jacket. By the way, I have no idea how to say "straight jacket" in Spanish, so that time, I admit, *estuve* compensating. *¿Y qué*, so what?

That's another thing. As Spanglish expands and standardizes, it generates its own idiomatic phrases like, "*Y qué*, so what." Which is technically redundant. You would never say, "*¿Y qué, y qué?*" or "So what, so what?" But somehow in Spanglish this is not only perfectly valid, it's become sort of a standard idiomatic expression, at least in New York, where my particular *tribu* of Spanglish speakers is from.

In case you're wondering, yes: *seguro que hay regionalismos*. But despite variations, Spanglish everywhere operates the same way. "*La troka,*" "*el* subway," same difference. *Llegarás* to where you're going. My girlfriend is Mexican and she has no trouble understanding my Puerto Rican grandmother's Spanglish. Or vice versa. *El único* glitch *es que mi abuelita* is losing her hearing and won't admit it, *lo cual* creates problems.

Just yesterday my girlfriend made the mistake of mentioning the term "hearing aid" to her. Now that, *por supuesto*, she heard and flipped out. "*Yo no me voy a poner ningún* hearing aid," she said, indignantly, in classic senior Spanglish. "*Pueden decir que yo soy orgullosa*, me don't care." I swear when I heard her say it, *por poco me muero de la risa*.

Obviously *mi abuelita* understood "hearing aid" in English. She's probably never even heard the term in Spanish, which is "*prótesis de oído amplificador.*" (I had to *googlear* it myself just now.) I'm sure none of her doctors and nurses and home attendants, *ni siquiera los que hablan español,* ever say it in Spanish. Why? *Pues,* it's easier not to. And everybody knows what you're talking about if you say it in English. In this country, *hasta los chinos* call it a "hearing aid" as a function of practicality.

Plus, switching out of Spanish to say "hearing aid" also gave my grandmother's first sentence a little extra "*¡fuácata!*" of protest at the end. The switch *por sí mismo* stresses her point. *Preferiría estar sorda* than walk around with a plastic *pendejada* in her ear.

In her second sentence, she repeats the same pattern: Spanish followed by an emphatic burst of English. And the "me don't care" is delivered *con un poquito de gracia* in her endearingly imperfect *inglés.* She knows it's cute. She may not have even been aware that she was switching languages, but she was trying to be funny, *y así le salió.*

Mucho Fun = *Mucho* Funny

Spanglish speakers intuitively revel in the playfulness of it. *¡Se goza un montón!* Have you ever watched sea otters frolicking in the sea *en el* Discovery Channel? Don't they look like they're having a blast? That's how much fun Spanglish speakers are having when enjoying *el chistoso juego de palabras* that the *habla* makes possible.

Other languages can convey humor, but the *habla* has got *mucho* funny already packed into it. *Por lo tanto,* Spanglish always breaks the ice. It's ideal for social occasions or even job interviews. One time I was applying *para un* part-time at Cuchifrito Corp. The owner asked me why I wanted the job. I said, "*Porque* because," and was hired on the spot. Part of the playfulness and humor of the language is facilitated by the freedom of it. "Twice the vocabulary and half the grammar," as I'm fond of pointing out, is a signature virtue of the *habla*, emancipating *nosotros los* Spanglishistas from official dos and don'ts. Ah, *pero* it's not so *fácil*. Below the surface, *operando a un nivel desapercibido*, there's a whole substrata of laws *dictando el* mix *para que cuadre perfectamente* every time.

An unfailing Spanglish ear allows us to integrate English and Spanish fluidly and organically. *A pesar de que todavía no haya una gramática oficialmente reconocida* for the *habla* yet, *sí existe una especie de* inner logic to it, innately possessed by native Spanglish speakers *y algunos gringo* savants.

Anticipation of something Spanglish *al punto de zafarse de tu boca* sets off an involuntary syntactical scramble to make it all fit together:

(a) The grammars *de ambos idiomas* have to be reconciled.

(b) *Se tiene que efectuar un* cross check *de palabras prestadas* against alternate language contexts *para asegurar* viability.

(c) *Hay que elegir el* Spanish-to-English ratio *más apropiado.*

(d) Juxtapositional compatability *en cada switcheo tiene que verificarse.*

(e) *El mejor* word order *se tiene que negociar.*

(f) Lexical stems *de un idioma* have to be tricked out *con los sufijos, los prefijos y las conjugaciones* of another, to supply *todas las palabritas* brand new.

(g) *Cada expresión tiene que someterse a un* pre-screening *riguroso,* to filter for authenticity over gratuitous affectation, *pero siempre con un* waiver for clever exaggerations *en son de broma.*

Ahora, one unwritten rule of the *habla* overrides all others. In the event of an emergency, *de repente* all systems go on red alert *para conseguir y disparar* the single most perfect word available in either language. That's why *puedes haber estado hablando* English all day, *pero cuando* you suddenly hit your thumb with a hammer, "*¡Coño!*" comes flying out of your mouth.

So you see, Spanglish *no se habla* willy-nilly. *Se rige por ciertas reglas subconscientes.* But ultimately it comes down to one question. Does it feel natural? Does it sound like Spanglish to the Spanglish ear? *Ahí está* the real test.

Bad Spanglish

I didn't realize how unnatural Spanglish could sound *hasta que un día* I was called in as a Spanglish consultant. An animated children's series was being developed for John Leguizamo, and I was hired to go through the script. They wanted me to correct the Spanglish. *¡Imagínate!* And let me tell you, it was some of the worst Spanglish I think I have ever been exposed to *en mi vida.*

I had a ginormous *problemo* with the whole script. On the first page one character, actually named "Spanglish," says, "Have you *perdiste* your mind?" This was so grating to my Spanglish ears, *que te juro que* they started bleeding. *Me sonó* worse *que veinte gatos afilándose las uñas* on a chalkboard.

Spanglish that bad just doesn't exist in nature. Not only did it sound unnatural. I also distinctly heard the fabric of the space-time continuum tearing. *Así de* ridiculously jarring *me sonó.* It violated all the internal Spanglish safety measures that would normally prevent such a heinous *disparate* from ever being formed.

First of all, "*perdiste*" is a reflexive conjugation of "*perder*," meaning it already implies the personal pronoun "*tú,*" or "you." *Es decir,* that's one too many, *mijo!* And the mistake lodges in your brain *como si fuera un* friggin' clot, one big *habla*-horrorific-hematoma. *El dolor que me causó era insoportable,* I swear. Also, there's no organic trigger prompting or justifying the switch. The Spanish *está* jammed into the sentence, *a las malas.* Any Spanish verb *en esa posición* simply wouldn't work *sin quedar sumamente* awkward. Obviously, it was written by a Spanglish *guánabi.*

Resulta que, just as I *sospeché,* the writer wasn't a native Spanglish-*hablante* but a Greek imposter who assumed *que podía* get by on her broken Greeklish. I wasn't surprised *porque la verdad es que* it sounded Greek to me. Anyway, *me la presentaron* and she asked me what I thought of the script. I said, "Have you *perdiste* your mind?" And I was fired on the spot.

Spreading *la Palabra* about the *Habla*

When I hear perfect Spanglish, *te digo que me emociona. Me dan* goosebumps *pero* all over. *En cambio, ejemplos* that diminish it, *y que* don't do the *habla* justice, *me vuelven loco.* Bad examples only embolden the anti-*habla* fundamentalists who believe Spanglish will eventually "make it *una* very *grande problemo to poder understandnos.*"

Well, *lo siento, pero* nobody actually talks like that. *Aunque* such a clunky construction is possible, it's clearly a *retardismo.* Anyone who tries to pass that off as legitimate Spanglish *te está bullshiteando.*

Mi gente deserve better. As a self-ordained Spanglish evangelist, I am doing what I can to change that, and spread *la palabra* about the *habla.*

Whenever I go into full-frontal Spanglish during a show, afterward someone always says, "That was hilarious, even though I didn't understand half of what you said!" So imagine *cómo de* funny *y emocionante debe de ser para* everybody who does understand it all. These are the folks who come up afterward *y me dicen,* "Oh my God, *¡así mismo es que habla mi familia!* Wow, *pero* seriously *te botaste! Estuvo* hilarious!"

That extra appreciation of the *habla* by native Spanglishistas, *quienes lo reconocen como* their own, is what makes it all worthwhile. And I've noticed something that never fails. On stage, as in my personal life, Spanglish *es tremendo para el* bonding.

A few words instantly let other Spanglishistas know that you share a kind of schizophrenic experience with them, in which Spanish and English can't exist without each other. So that as pervasive and mainstream as Spanglish is *hoy en día*, for us it still serves as a sort of a sentimental inside joke. Only, *no estamos jokeando*. It communicates *nuestra verdadera* reality.

Si yo tuviera que escoger between English and Spanish, *sería un* tough choice. They each represent a distinct identity. But Spanglish speakers are not one or the other. *Somos* both. Spanglish lets me speak both, inhabit both, be both, *a la misma vez*.

The *habla* also preserves identity. Upwardly mobile Latinos often rely on Spanglish to counter the negative effects of assimilation, such as *volviéndose demasiado gringo*. Every word of *español* they can throw out into an English-speaking environment is a little victory for who they are on the inside. Even just slipping in a "*bendito*" or two at the office is a personal act of lingual *reconquista*. By the way, my spellcheck just tried to change the word "*bendito*" to "bandito." *Para que vean* what we're up against.

Spanglish Around *El Mundo*

But as much as we claim Spanglish as our own in the United States, it is constantly becoming more global.

In Spain, where there are legions of Spanglish speakers *en el closet*, they call jogging, "*hacer el footing.*" And "bungee jumping" has mutated beyond recognition. The English suffix "ing" gets tagged onto "*puente*," the Spanish word for bridge (where apparently most Spanish *bungistas* are jumping from), to beget "*puenting.*" Of course, if you bungee-jump while playing *timbales*, it's called "*tito-puenting.*"

In Argentina, *donde la gente se enorgullece tanto de hablar un castellano* super *culto*, instead of saying "*auspicio*" or "*patrocinio*" to mean "sponsorship," the Spanglish term "*esponsoreo*" does the trick. The *habla* is becoming so popular *con los argentinos*, I'm thinking of going down there to offer some "*sin barreras*" type of Spanglish crash courses in exchange for tango lessons. So don't be surprised if one day you see me win it all in a live broadcast of the World Tango Championships, brought to you by "*el esponsoreo de Espanglish Sin Vergüenza.*"

In Gibraltar, a sort of Galapagos Island of Spanglish, where the *habla* has evolved in relative isolation, we find some unique specimens. The Spanish verb "*disfrutar*," meaning "to enjoy," is being enjoyed in a whole new way. When making plans for the evening, Gibraltans say, "Let's go out and really '*disfrute*' ourselves tonight." *En este caso el español ha sido* Englishized! Clearly, Spanglish has taken root on the Rock.

In Canada, *me quedé en* shock *encontrarme con un* fellow Spanglishista working the cash register at McDonald's and handing me back change in the local funny money. "*Disculpe todos los* loonies, eh," she said. "*Pero es que* I'm all out of toonies." I had no idea she was talking about *dinero*.

Separated at Birth?

Yet *el español* is only one of the many languages *alrededor del mundo* combining *de forma semejante* with English. There's Hinglish, Chinglish (a.k.a. Engrish), Japlish, Tagalish, Singlish, Poglish, Deutschlish, and Franglais, just to name a few "lishes." And many of those are also *bastante corrientes en los Estados Unidos.* How does the *habla* stack up against the competition? Well, obviously, I'm partial and think *que entre todos los* "lishes," Spanglish is the most delish.

Pero what distinguishes Spanglish most is the critical mass *del fenómeno* in this country. There are roughly three billion Spanglish speakers in my grandmother's building alone, *según los últimos* figures.

From a historical perspective, *debemos tener en cuenta también que* Spanish was here first. By first, I mean before English. By here, I mean *el norte.* In fact, there's evidence that when Ponce de León landed in Florida, the natives he "discovered" were already fans of Ricky Martin. He's older than he looks.

Now add to that another important element, proximity to *la patria.* The homelands of most Latinos who have come to the United States are incredibly close by. Puerto Rico is just a subway ride away. It's the second-to-last stop on the A Train. (*Pero si está* running local, bring a book *porque* it can take a while.) People swim here from Cuba all the time. Dominicans *se esconden* in the wheel wells *de los aviones* and hold on for the trip.

Mexicans, and all the other Central and South Americans coming through Mexico pretending to be Mexicans, can walk (and jump and run) right across the border. Not to mention all those immigrants who never even had to immigrate, because they already lived in Texas and Arizona and New Mexico and Utah and Colorado and Nevada and California, a region still shown as "occupied Mexico" on some maps.

And *hablando de todo un poco*, have you taken a look at a U.S. map lately? Half the places in this country still have Spanish names. And would someone please put the *ñ* back in Montana? I was just there and got tired of telling everybody it should be *Montaña*.

The city of Chicago, in fact, was named by its Spanglish-speaking founder, in honor of his wife, who refused to leave him no matter how much he always begged her, "*Chica*, go."

Other "lishes" haven't made that kind of an imprint here. I hear Filipinos in San Francisco all the time mixing Tagalog and English. But how many U.S. cities, towns, roads, and waterways have Tagalog names? How many Tagalog *palabras* are there in the English dictionary? How many non-Filipino Americans know the words to at least one Tagalog song? What's the Tagalog equivalent of "*Feliz Navidad*"?

Spanish (and therefore Spanglish) has a special foothold in this country. It's ubiquitous coast to coast and is a champion *idioma* in its own right worldwide. Of course the undisputed heavyweight language of the world is English, a title previously held by Latin and Sanskrit. And before that by Cavemantalk, which consisted of mostly grunting and the occasional interjection of "Awesome!" and "*¡Chévere!*" In the end it was just spoken by one guy named Og Hernández, who used to mumble to himself a lot.

This *y otras coincidencias* suggest that English and Spanish *pudieron haber evolucionado* from the same proto-language. *Qué* trippy, *¿verdad?* In other words, Spanglish could be a reunification of two languages separated at *nacimiento*. *Las investigaciones* are ongoing. *Pero esta teoría* would explain why, *hoy en día*, English and Spanish zip together so well into Spanglish.

This perfect blendship is a beautiful thing to behold. Normally *los idiomas* startup *crecen poco a poco*, taking their sweet time getting off the ground. *Pero en comparación*, Spanglish *está arrancando como un* bat out of hell.

We have a front row seat at the birth of a homegrown language, exploding *de una manera alucinante* right before our very eyes, *y más al grano*, our ears. It's the way all languages naturally form, only faster than ever before. *Debemos aprovechar.* It's a rare opportunity to enjoy, contribute, evaluate, and learn from such a spectacular unfolding.

Can I get a witness? "*¡Cójelo con* take it easy, amen!*"

Now I realize not everybody shares my *entusiasmo* for the *habla*. Hopefully by the end of this book, however, I can sway you sniveling *zánganos* to see things my way. If not, we can always settle this *mano a mano*. Can you say *lucha libre*, boys and girls? I'd be more than happy to defend my views in a no-holds-barred Spanglish-*o-muerte* smackdown.

Why? *¡Porque because!*

TOP TEN SPANGLISH BUMPER STICKERS

1. MY OTHER CAR *ES UNA PORQUERÍA TAMBIÉN*

2. HONK *SI ERES INDOCUMENTADO*

3. I'D RATHER BE *HABLANDO ESPAÑOL*

4. *PENDEJO* ON BOARD

5. *AMIGOS* DON'T LET *AMIGOS* EAT TACO BELL

6. *¿ESTAMOS* THERE YET*?*

7. IF YOU CAN READ THIS BUMPER STICKER, *ESTÁS MUY* CLOSE

8. ALIENS ARE FROM MARS. *YO SOY DE MICHOACÁN*

9. *CHANGÓ* IS MY CO-PILOT

10. FORGET MILK, *DAME MÁS GASOLINA*

BONUS: *YO* ♥ SPANGLISH. TWICE THE VOCABULARY. HALF THE GRAMMAR.

— 3 —

LOS RULES

OF ENGAGEMENT

I may be dead, *pero todavía estoy* horny.
—epitaph on the tomb of the unknown *mujeriego*

Until now the rules of Spanglish have been unwritten. And, *para ser sincero*, many would have preferred they stay that way. Yet somehow I managed to succeed where *tantos habían fracasado* before me.

Not that I am any fan of grammar. The more I try to learn it, *cuanto más* paranoid *me pongo* that I'm not qualified to be communicating in any language. Seriously, *todos mis* textbooks *viejos* are full of ridiculously hard to follow explanations, *como la siguiente*:

> Any spastical pronoun persuant to the full frontal interrogatory negation of the infinitive garfunkel should always face Mecca relative to the extra nuclear flying monkeys in the third down of the main clause when followed by a double helix in the falsetto voice deriving tangentially but not passively every other Wednesday from the indirect object of the antecedent marsupial.

¡Olvídate! That's *muy* confusing. And, *te lo juro*, that's exactly what all that nonsense sounds like to me. *¡No, hombre, no!* I said to myself, *mejor* to start *desde* scratch.

Bueno, this totally liberated me to discover *cuáles son los* dos and don'ts *de un* language you aren't even supposed to be speaking in the first place. The research is ongoing. *Pero*, I can't wait to share with you *mis conclusiones* so far.

There are hundreds and hundreds of Spanglish rules, and new ones pop up every day as research continues at the Santiago Spanglish Institute for World Peace. *Sin embargo*, as space is *medio*-limited, and this book is contractually obligated to entertain, I've selected *algunos de los* rules *más entretenidos* to help whet your Spanglish whistle.

Aparecen aquí in the same random order *que se escogieron para ser* included.

SPANGLISH RULE #18

Never say hips when you mean *caderas*.

Words don't always mean the same thing even when they supposedly do. So make sure to switch languages whenever doing so facilitates accuracy.

I mean, if you look up the word "hips" in an English/Spanish dictionary, it will tell you the correct word in Spanish is *caderas*. But that is, *como se dice*, way off. *Caderas* means "hips," but so much more than "hips." Just look at the two. Even the word *caderas* seems to have more *caderas* than the word "hips."

First of all, *caderas* has a gender, and that gender is female, which gives the word extra superpowers when referring to a female.

Also, notice that you can describe hips as curvaceous. But the word *caderas* already implies that. Curvaceous *caderas* would be redundant, although they do exist (especially in Brazil). Plus, *caderas* has three syllables, instead of just one, giving it built-in motion. When pronounced correctly, the word even has a syncopation to it, so that when you hear it, you picture those *caderas* dancing or making love.

Of course, everybody knows Shakira had that hit song "Hips Don't Lie." Yeah, well, let me put it to you this way. You will tell any lie necessary for *caderas*. That's *la diferencia*.

SPANGLISH RULE #509

Love bastard words as if they were your own.

Bastardization of vocabulary *es muy esencial* to Spanglish. In fact, most of what people recognize as Spanglish refers to such bastardized beauties as *furnitura*, a Spanishized form of the English word "furniture." Easy, right? A little spelling change at the end to make it sound Spanish-sounding, *y estás* good to go. *Claro que* the correct Spanish word for "furniture" is "*muebles*." But everybody knows if you want a good deal, look for a *furnitura* sale at a reputable *furnituría*, with a sign in the window that says, "*Hacemos* delivery."

Note that bastard words are usually the ones that make you laugh the most, because they strike you as so odd and out of place and clearly wrong. Which is also what makes them feel *tan* right to *nosotros* die-hard connoisseurs of the *habla*.

I just heard this one in Chicago, and it's still cracking me up. Instead of saying, "I like" something, advanced Spanglish speakers there say, "*Me likea.*" For instance:

"Do you like your tequila?"

"Sí, me likea mi tequila."

C'mon now, *les digo que* I just laughed again *a carcajadas* as I typed it. How can you not *likear* a word like "*likea*"?

What about reverse bastardization? Happens all the time. *Cuántas veces* haven't you heard a cowboy *en una película* western saying *algo como*, "He vamoosed with all the *dinero*" or "Vamoose fellas!" or "Better vamoose"?

Well, did you think any of these involved an actual moose? Of course not. It's simply an Americanized form of the Spanish word *vamos*, which *vaqueros* in a hurry say to mean "let's go," "scram," "beat it," or "skedaddle."

Now, I have a doctor friend just learning Spanish who likes to put her own twist on it. When it's time to vamoose, she says, "Shall we *vamos*?" It's more polite and endearingly more wrong to my Spanglish ears.

SPANGLISH RULE #110

Thou shalt conjugate English words into Spanish.

This is taking bastardization to the next level, and *sin lugar a dudas* it is one of the fluent Spanglish speaker's most basic instincts. Almost as if it were involuntary, *nosotros* Spanglish speakers *kidnapeamos* English words from their realms and slap Spanish verb tenses on the end of them, *como si no tuviera nada de extraño.*

Lo hacemos as if we didn't know they weren't *palabras españolas* to begin with! *Pero esta costumbre* makes us more fun to *janguear* with.

In case you didn't recognize it, *janguear* is Spanglish for "to hang out." We really make this one our own. First we change the spelling to reflect Spanish *pronunciación.* And then we conjugate the hell out of the bastard, without asking anybody permission: *Yo jangueo, tú jangueas, él/ella janguea, nosotros jangueamos,* ellos *janguean* . . . And if addressing upper-crust Spanglishistas, you might even say, *vosotros jangueáis.*

What's more, the word has been adopted into the official municipal lexicon in some Los Angeles neighborhoods, where I have actually seen street signs to discourage loitering that say, "*No Janguear.*"

And notice that *janguear* is used only for that one connotation of "to hang." You would never greet anybody with, "Hey, how's it *jangueando?*"

Now, you can also conjugate Spanish words to give them English endings, but no examples come to mind. *Estoy* totally blanking. I'll have to get *pensar-*ing on this one.

SPANGLISH RULE #32

Never, *pero nunca nunca,* stay in English or Spanish too long, *que da mal ejemplo.*

You must switch between languages compulsively, *casi* pathologically, *si quieres hacerte* master *del idioma* Spanglish. *Ahí está la cosa.* What makes Spanglish come alive, *más que cualquier otro detalle*, is that constant *switcheo.* *Tienes que* go for it every time, *siempre y cuando* the switch is in compliance with Spanglish dos and don'ts—which, frankly, *todavía están* up for grabs.

The seasoned Spanglish *hablante* is on the lookout for any chance to switch, *como un gato medio* wild *buscando* any chance to slip out of the house. If the door is left open just a crack . . . it's *hasta la vista* baby.

SPANGLISH RULe #60

Wherever there's junction, Spanglish will function.

Listen to Spanglish closely, *y te fijarás que* a lot of the switching tends to happen *justo cuando* one phrase or fragment or clause, or other unit of speech or thought, links or transitions to the next. (Think commas, periods, prepositions, and conjunction words!)

Aim to switch at these lingual *encrucijadas*, intuitively reconciling the gramars *del inglés y el español* for perfect fit and maximum flow *en lo que brincas* back and forth. Trust me, *una vez que* you get the hang of it, you'll wonder *por qué tardaste tanto* to start doing it.

Each one of these junctures can function as a revolving door into either language.

Por ejemplo, you can be going along in English, English—blah blah blah—

then throw in a *pero*, which takes you instantly into *español*. Or you might be speaking *en español, español*—blah blah blah—*y de repente te tiras un* "but," *que te conduce muy fácilmente* into English.

Por cierto, that's exactly how Spanglish actually sounds to people who don't understand both languages. Half the time it's just *mucho* blah blah blah.

SPANGLISH RULE #7

Put approved English words *a trabajar en tu español*.

Approved English words are words that have not yet been adopted officially into Spanish, *sin embargo* they thrive there, *a consecuencia de* popular usage and abusage.

Think of these approved English words as having guest-worker visas to operate in your Spanish here in the United States, a.k.a., the Spanglish homeland. *Nótese que* outside the homeland, *tal uso* is more illegal but no less frequent.

Estas palabras inglesas are generally underpaid *pero muy trabajadoras*, so please employ them as much as possible. *Aunque sea sólo* part-time.

Just how many of these approved English words are there currently? Roughly, *un montón*. Other estimates put the number closer to a *montón* and a half. But, *por ahora*, we'll look at just a few.

Spanglish Shortlist of *Palabras Aprobadas del Inglés*

OFF

I'm not hung over. *Pero me siento un poco* off.

Apaga la televisión. Don't make me say it again. *¡Ponla* off!

Esa mujer en el front row, *anoche,* laughed her *nalgas* off.

El goofing off *es un mecanismo de* coping.

They recycle everything, *y viven muy* off *la* grid.

Don't set the alarm *que mañana tengo el día* off.

Try to make it, *que la fiesta va a estar* off the hook.

APPOINTMENT

Hice un appointment *en la* beauty *para darme un nuevo* look.

I can't now, *porque tengo un* appointment to have a fight with my wife.

Oh, he's too busy to talk to his friends. *Hay que hacer un* appointment.

Pero si hoy no hacemos el teeth whitening. *Su* appointment *era pa'* yesterday.

Tuve un appointment with myself *para ir* shopping *en* Victoria's Secret.

COMPLAIN

Yo no me paso complaining *de nada.*

Mi único complain *es que* she snores like a horse.

OK, *tengo un* complain *para tí. ¿Por qué no estoy en tu* Top 8 *de* MySpace?

The concert sucked. *Mucha gente estaba* complaining about *el* lipsynching.

Sorry about your haircut. *Métele un* complain *al* Better Business Bureau.

DOWN

After I gained the weight back, *me sentí bien* down.

Mija, those diamonds were fake. *Son* 15 *dólares que se fueron* down the drain.

The guy *se ve muy amable, muy* down on earth, *¿no?*

So are we all going to Puerto Rico for Christmas? *Porque* I'm down!

We turned off the lights. *Entonces le di un beso en el* downtown.

FULL

Perdóname, my bad. *Acepto* full responsibility.

Es que I can't eat another bite. *Ya estoy* full.

Después de ser una ama de casa full-time *por tantos años*, I'm really enjoying *estar divorciada*.

¿Cómo de full *está la clase de* spinning?

Ese Lou *"El Gordo"* Dobbs on CNN *es tan arrogante, tan presumido, tan* full of himself.

HOMELESS

Throw them out already, *que ni un* homeless *se pone esos zapatos*.

Estoy harto de estar schlepping* around, *como si fuera un* homeless.

If you don't, *por lo menos*, get *un* part–time, *nos quedamos* homeless.

I'm telling you, *ese hombre* homeless drives *un* Cadillac Escalade *nuevecito*.

¿Vivir contigo? Prefiero estar homeless.

SERIOUS

Tengo algo super serious *que discutir contigo* about *esas mini faldas* you like to wear.

---

*Note the word *schlepping* here. Yiddish goes very well with Spanglish; experts consider the blend a kind of postmodern Sephardic bodega-bonics.

Seriously, *no es pa' tanto.*

He'll never win the *tamale*-eating contest, *hasta que no se ponga* serious.

But like seriously, *te lo digo,* I totally blanked.

Gracias a Dios, it was just a rash, *nada muy* serious.

SHOW

Basta ya de estar fooling around. *¡Se acabó el* show!*

Ah no, *esta familia es un* show!

No voy a poder ir a tu show, *pero te deseo mucho* luck.

Siempre le gusta estar showing off.

Como quien dice, "El show *tiene que* go on."

SPANGLISH RULE #19

Every Spanglish journey *comienza con una sola palabra.*

*Hint: Remember to pronounce the *sh* in "show" with a *ch* sound, as in *choo-choo.*

Tweaking a sentence at either end with just one word of *inglés* or *español* gives Spanglish speakers endless *posibilidades*. Notice each group of examples below has an entirely different feel based on the placement of the one word that is, *como se decía en* Sesame Street, "not like the others."

SENTENCES IN SPANISH ENDING WITH AN ENGLISH WORD

Afuera está pouring.

¡Me quedé en shock!*

Algunos doctores son medio clueless.

La verdad que fue un bummer.

Hay que aprender el tricky.

SENTENCES IN ENGLISH ENDING WITH A SPANISH WORD

I'm here waiting for the damn bus *todavía*.

If you're not serious about divorce, don't get me all *entusiasmado*.

She is in incredibly good shape for a *cuarentona*.

Oh, he can jumpstart anything with a motor *fácilmente*.

I'm new at strip-dominoes, so take it easy *conmigo*.

SENTENCES IN ENGLISH STARTING WITH
A SPANISH WORD

Ahora things are gonna get personal.

Son retarded looking.

Déjame page him again, OK?

Algo's not right with the President.

Regresaremos right after these messages.

SENTENCES IN SPANISH STARTING WITH
ONE ENGLISH WORD

Stay *hasta que se vaya el chupacabras.*

Lately, *estoy soñando mucho con Shakira.*

Pray *que te pegues en la loto.*

Maybe *tenía una chilla por ahí.*

Shave *porque con esa barba sólo te besa el perro.*

See what I mean about how the placement of the alternate language word totally shapes the expression?

Ending a Spanish sentence with an English word punches it up with a last-second surprise. You get fooled into thinking the entire sentence is going to be *en español* and then "Bam!" Spanglish speakers often favor this technique for its quirky playfulness.

Ending an English sentence with a Spanish word is a more gentle reversal, usually signaling that beneath the English dialogue lurks the heart of an incorrigible Spanish speaker who likes to sneak *nuestro idioma* in wherever he or she can. It's a very flavorful finish.

Kicking off an English sentence with one Spanish word—whoa, that is balls-out Spanglish, very pro-active *bilingüismo*. This technique gives the whole rest of the sentence a Spanish feel—almost an accent!

Starting a Spanish sentence off with an English word is a real attention grabber, cutting through the clutter and hooking people in for what is about to suddenly become a *Telemundo* moment. This technique always catches people off guard and is the Spanglish equivalent of pitching a slider.

Now go back and read the examples again so that this rule really sinks in. *Sé que lo ibas a hacer* anyway.

SPANGLISH RULE #213

There's no such thing as *demasiado* redundant or too *repetitivo*.

In the effort to be understood, Spanglish speakers *no se toman* chances. In fact, *cuando tengas cualquier* doubt, always make a point of being redundant to cover all your bases.

Here's the first example that comes to mind:

¿*Vas a subir* upstairs?

This is a strange one. But I hear it all the time. And it illustrates a very common feature of the *habla*.

In this case there's a clear overlap in meaning because the verb *subir* means "to climb (up)." *¡No te puedes subir* down!* So when you say "*subir* upstairs," there's an extra "up" in there!

Pero, just do it, *y no te vayas a poner* hung up about the extra "up."

Sometimes the redundancies are more blatant, as in the following examples. *Como verán*, they merely consist of a word or phrase *seguida por su traducción*. But in Spanglish, *el conjunto aparece* as a single unit sharing one meaning.

> **Maybe** *a lo mejor*
>
> *A ver* **we'll see**
>
> **Please** *por favor*
>
> *A veces* **sometimes**
>
> *Te digo* **I'm telling you**
>
> **Almost** *por poco*
>
> *Te lo juro* **I swear**

Each of these couplets appears regularly in Spanglish and they have become idioms inherent to the *habla*. Memorize them. Use them. And see how many new ones you can make up on your own.

¿Qué qué? You actually thought I forgot about "*Cójelo con* take it easy"? *¡Jamás!* It's just that it is such a special case of redundancy *que requiere un análisis mucho más* in-depth.

So please *por favor, diríjanse a la página* 121.

SPANGLISH RULE #141

Beware of *mijo* mania.

Take it easy with the *mijos, mijo*. There's nothing wrong with a *mijo* or *mija* here and there *en moderación*, or authentically woven into *lo que estés diciendo, mija*. But too often, *la gente se luce* and it's *mijo* this and *mija* that all over the place with no other Spanish in between.

I'm not pointing any *dedos, mijo*. But you know who you are. *Así que*, learn some self-control, *mijo*, and some more Spanish. *¡Por-fa-vor!*

Dialogue *escrito para personajes* latinos in English-language books and movies, *por ejemplo*, is chock-full of *mijos* and *mijas*. This is done to add *un toquecito de realismo*, but it mostly reeks of clueless pandering and *tokenismo, mija*.

Mijo and *mija*, of course, are contractions of *mi hijo* and *mi hija*, meaning "my son" and "my daughter," respectively. They can be used by anybody, though, as terms of endearment. For instance: "This is a hold-up, *mijo*."

De repente, it's also become a very trendy crossover hook. A friend of mine even started a magazine called *Mija*. And what could I say but, "You go, *mija!*"

SPANGLISH RULE #876:

Your Spanglish is only as good as your last *frase idiomática*.

Idioms always win. In the tug of war between English and Spanish in the brain of a Spanglish *hablante*, the strongest tug *siempre vendrá* from the biggest, baddest idiom, the alpha idiom, the idiom on steroids. *Lo mismo* goes for clichés and colloquialisms.

For example: "*Estoy teniendo un* bad hair day."

In the above case, the savvy Spanglish speaker switched out of Spanish to accommodate an expression that exists only in English: "Bad hair day." You will never hear anyone in Spanish complaining about having "*un día de cabello malo.*" Apparently, in Spanish, either you have good hair on your head or you don't. It's a more permanent concept, not subject to daily fluctuations.

Las frases idiomáticas en español can have that same effect, also triggering *un cambio de idioma* in the other direction.

For example: "She wanted to get married a virgin, and then *metió la pata.*"

The phrase "*meter la pata*" means roughly, "to blow it big time," often in a sexual context, as in "to become pregnant" or "to impregnate."

Literally translated it means "to put your leg in it." But people always translate it into English as "to put your foot in it." I guess in Spanish, *como los latinos somos tan exagerados*, putting in just your foot wouldn't get you into any trouble. *Tiene que ser* the whole leg.

And another thing, *pata* is the Spanish word for an animal's leg. Humans have *piernas*, not *patas*. So you even lose your human status in the deal! Either way, it's understood as a euphemism for screwing up royally or falling from grace morally. And it's not just a Puerto Rican thing. I did some fact checking. I asked my girlfriend, who is Mexican, and it rang a bell with her too. She recalled, laughing, "My parents never said, 'Don't have sex.' It was always, '*No vayas a meter la pata.*'"

If you ever want to know *quien ha metido la pata* lately, just ask *mi abuelita*. Not only is she keeping tabs. "*Meter la pata*" is one of her favorite phrases *cuando* she's in *chisme* mode. Naturally, it's the more risqué connotations, *en cuanto al sexo y el embarazo*, that really crack her up.

Spanglish speakers have the advantage of being able to switch back and forth so as not to lose any idiomatic flavor in translation. *Por lo tanto*, only in Spanglish can you *meter la pata* and have *un* bad hair day *a la misma vez*.

SPANGLISH RULE #33

No te preocupes, be trigger happy!

Language switches are often instinctual or conditioned responses to Spanglish stimuli. Let these triggers ping and pong you between *los universos paralelos de* English and Spanish.

Estos llamados triggers are found *en un sin número de variedades*. They can be emotional, psychological, physical, contextual, aesthetic, environmental, or *simplemente* practical in nature.

Essentially, they cause linguistic reflex actions *al estilo* Pavlov, just like blinking or salivating or telling a telemarketer *que no fastidie más, ¡maldito sea!* Often, once a speaker is triggered to switch into English or Spanish, he or she will stay in that language until triggered to switch again.

Veamos algunos ejemplos.

EJEMPLO #1

He forgot my birthday. *Ni siquiera una llamada.*
(emotional trigger, switch prompted by jolt of indignation)

EJEMPLO #2

Yo nunca me pierdo porque **I mapquest everything.**
(practical trigger, switch prompted by decision to use tech-savvy lingo)*

EJEMPLO #3

That was last week. *No me hable de* **last week.**
(psychological trigger, switch prompted by desire to move on from the past/then a switch back prompted by inability to let go)

---

*Note: The switch into English here is made on the word "I" in anticipation of the internet term "mapquest," used here as a verb. This Spanglish speaker knew better than to say "yo mapquest everything" or "yo mapquesteo everything"—both of which would have sounded weird and much more unnatural. A good Spanglish ear won't permit this kind of desgracia. So the speaker switches in such a way to accommodate the target English term and facilitate natural conversational flow via a compatible grammatical route. I know you had no idea there was that much going on. ¡Es que nosotros Spanglish speakers somos muy complicados!

EJEMPLO #4

Tan pronto yo siento dolor, I pop a Tylenol.
(over-the-counter trigger, switch prompted by migraine)

EJEMPLO #5

"¡Mira, ahí lo dice! Wrong way!"
(visual trigger, switch prompted by wish not to hit oncoming traffic)

SPANGLISH RULE #16

A veces se nos antoja un **sandwich.**

A great way to get your Spanglish on is to sandwich English and Spanish *dentro de nuestras conversaciones* as parenthetical phrases. This lends a sense of balance and a certain aesthetic *equilibrio.* Experiment with embedding *inglés dentro del español* and vice versa.

SPANGISH, ENGLISH, SPANISH

"Estaba sola en casa, minding my own business, cuando sonó el teléfono . . . "
—My friend Nelly, recalling the night *que metió la pata* and got pregnant *con su hijo* Zachy

ENGLISH, SPANISH, ENGLISH

"Seriously, *aunque no lo parezca*, it's true."

—Me, insisting that I am a highly organized person

ENGLISH, SPANISH, ENGLISH

"I'm telling you, *aquí, lo que ella dice*, goes."

—Papi, about who wears the *pantalones* in our family

SPANGLISH RULE #155

Acuérdense to vary your English/*español* ratio.

Varying the ratio of English to Spanish will make your Spanglish more dynamic and believable.

Try lots of Spanish with a little English, alternating with lots of English *con un chipitito de español*. Maybe go half and half for a while. Or *quédense* entirely in one language for a stretch, *si les parece apropiado*.

Keep in mind that a perfect 50/50 ratio between English and Spanish does have a magical quality—when it occurs spontaneously. But never force it. *Suena ridículo.*

For example, *jamás sería recomendable* to switch languages mechanically *cada otra palabra.*

Déjenme show you why:

Estuve shopping *por* hours *ayer* looking *por* a *nuevo* pair *de* dancing *zapatos* to *ponerme* Saturday *noche*. ¿Are *tú* also *yendo* to *ese* Fifth *de* May *fiesta* at *el* pub *Piedra* of Blarney *en* Irish *plaza?* Maybe *podemos* go *juntos.*

Nobody talks like that, *tan chapuceado!* I mean, *qué* clunky, *¿no?* Spanglish shouldn't sound *como si fuera* generated by a software virus.

Distribute your *inglés y español* leisurely and naturally over the course of a conversation, letting the ratio fluctuate, *pero de manera que no resulte en un* Spanglish *vergonzoso.*

SPANGLISH RULE #21

Say *adiós* to sexless persons, places, and things.

Because nearly everything *en español* is either masculine or feminine, as a Spanglish *hablante,* you get to sex up your English too. *Mediante este* gender assignment *lingüístico,* you can have a ball *animando instantáneamente* otherwise neutral *sustantivos.*

Cuando combinas a gender-neutral English noun *con un* gender-specific Spanish *artículo,* whether definite (*el, la, los, las*) or indefinite (*un, una, unos, unas*), you definitely add *un poquito de gracia* to *cualquier expresión.*

Permítanme ofrecerles a few *ejemplos:*

una runny nose

una friend *con* benefits

un power *lonche*

un rip off

unos fat deposits

el trailer

el restraining order

la Walmart

los munchies

Ah-ha! You see *de lo que estoy* talking about? With Spanglish, pick a gender, *y verán la diferencia.*

SPANGLISH RULE #702 (A)

Two personal pronouns are better than one.

One *muy* handy way to switch *entre inglés y español* is by employing the old personal pronoun redundancy trick. It has never been identified or revealed anywhere else ever before. *Es más, este próximo secreto que voy a compartir aquí con ustedes, solito vale el precio del libro, aún en* hardcover.

Simply repeat the same personal pronoun twice, back to back. Only the second time *asegúrate de que* it's in the alternate language: (. . . *él*, he . . .) or (. . . *ella*, she . . .) or (. . . he, *él* . . .) or (. . . she, *ella* . . .). Trust me, *estos* redundancy couplets *trabajan* brilliantly! Here are some examples of *el* tricky tricky in use:

> *Ay bendito, es que ella,* she's a ballbuster.

> I doubt *que tenga hambre porque* he, *él ya se hartó de* gummy bears.

> *Cuando ese* pitbull *baboso* got on the elevator, *nosotros,* we jumped the hell out.

> *Chico, es que yo,* I can't read other people's frickin' minds, *tú sabes.*

I know, I know, you never noticed it before! But it's so true, right? Throw this into your bag of tricks for hours of *mucho funno.*

SPANGLISH RULE #45

Be colorful and cross-modify.

Go out of your way to modify English and Spanish words with words from the other language. These combinations pack amazing creativity into just a pair of words, *y además demuestran la capacidad descriptiva inigualable del* Spanglish.

Efectuando la simbiosis perfecta between English and Spanish, cross–modification *te deja* show off *tu idioma de barbaridades* at its simple best. *Veamos estos ejemplos*:

> *Tenía una* tire *media* flat.
>
> After filling all those piñatas with condoms, *deberías estar* super *cansada*.
>
> Better make that two pizzas, *que tengo una hambre* heavy.
>
> Whoever pulled off that bank robbery had major *cojones*.
>
> They gave all the *viejitos* running the marathon "*Cana* Power!" T-shirts.

Réquete-cool, huh? Cross-modification *es nada menos que un* Spanglish force-multiplier. *Confío en que se aprovechen de esta técnica*—daily *y* flagrantly—*para que puedan* make it your own.

SPANGLISH RULE #623

Tienes que know *tus* Spanglish options.

Let me show you, *mis queridos lectores,* how the Spanglish ear sorts among a variety of combinations *para escojer* how to say something in the *habla.* As you progress along your Spanglish journey, analyzing these options becomes instinctual *y más sofisticado.* But *más les vale* getting to know the process *cuanto antes.*

Here are five different ways of Spanglishizing *el siguiente proverbio:* If you can't say something nice, don't say anything.

> 1. *Si no puedes decir nada* nice, *cállate la boca.*
>
> 2. If you can't say anything nice, *cállate la boca.*
>
> 3. If you can't say anything nice, keep your *boca* shut.
>
> 4. If you can't say anything nice, *no digas nada.*
>
> 5. If you can't say *nada* nice, shut your taco hole.

Technically, they all work. *Pero vamos a considerar* each one *en más detalle* and compare their relative (*por más* subjective *que sean*) merits.

1. *Si no puedes decir nada* nice, *cállate la boca.*

This one feels the most natural to me, because the word "nice" gives just the right *toquecito* of Spanglish for the job. It's not too heavy-handed. And I like how "*cállate la boca*" replaces "don't say anything" as a genuine and funnier Spanish idiom. It's funnier because it shifts the meaning to "shut your mouth," which could come off as *demasiado severo*, except that it's clearly done to be amusing.

Además, acuérdense que "nice" *es una palabra que se utiliza* so often *en español* by Spanglish speakers, *que ya casi se considera* a Spanish word (*por ejemplo: bien* nice, *qué* nice, *estuvo* nice, *qué tipo más* nice, etc.).

And I almost forgot *algo muy clave*, this one also features the couplet "*nada* nice," which gets bonus points for alliteration.

2. If you can't say anything nice, *cállate la boca*.

This one is OK. It breaks cleanly, *mostrando un switcheo* between clauses, *y también se aprovecha del humor* of the Spanish idiom. *Pero no sé*, I just don't feel *que* the word "nice" is getting as much pop as it would *si estuviera rodeado por el español* on both sides.

3. If you can't say anything nice, keep your *boca* shut.

My Spanglish ear would never allow me to drop the word "*boca*" completely out of nowhere into a sentence like that, *al menos que no fuera* on purpose as an affectation. For me, as a Spanish speaker, the phrase "*cállate la boca*," has such a strong internal cohesion as an idiom (and early childhood flashback), that my brain *evitaría* breaking it apart by switching *idiomas* within that phrase.

I wouldn't say "keep *tu boca* shut," either, or "keep your *boca cerrada*."

That's too forced, labored, and inorganic. In comparison, the word "nice" in that first example wasn't inserted arbitrarily but was left in, exactly *dónde* it originally appeared.

4. If you can't say anything nice, *no digas nada.*

This is a fairly literal half-and-half translation, *y por lo tanto* not very *divertido* at all.

5. If you can't say *nada* nice, shut your taco hole.

Aquí tenemos a very gringo-based *mezcla.* It converts "pie hole," American slang for "mouth," into "taco hole," giving it an ethnic twist. It's a fun (albeit potentially pejorative) play on *palabras.*

The only Spanish word is *nada,* betraying a deeper gringoness. I'd probably throw in a little more Spanish to keep the *"nada"* company, *porque no me cuesta nada.*

That said, to my Spanglish ears, this whole "taco hole" example would never pass the authenticity test. *Me suena tan pero tan* wrong. But what do I lose by playing around with it here to make a point? Absolutely *nada.*

SPANGLISH RULE #415:

Get buko bonus points for alliteration.

Spanglish benefits from playful sound combinations. Usually, *ésto ocurre sin pensarlo.* Just be open to it *y verás* how often *tus palabras combinarán* spontaneously to score bonus points for alliteration, as in *los siguientes ejemplos*:

> *Qué* clunky *baila ese tipo.*

> Hurry up, *¡apúrate puta!*

> Boy, what a *bocaful* of bull.

> *Esa Soledad es* super *simpática.*

> I can't move. *Estoy estoqueado.*

Fitting words together *de tal manera* makes them sound *como que* they were *casi* meant to be lexical *colaboradores, animando tu* Spanglish *con un toquecito de* poetic energy.

SPANGLISH RULE #28

Estar or not to *estar* (there's no question).

Hamlet would have had double trouble in Spanish, because *en el español* there are two words for the verb "to be." They are *estar* and *ser.*

So his dilemma *hubiera sido* both existential and semantic, especially if he didn't know the difference between transitive and intransitive verbs (and who does?).

But Spanglish speakers choose *estar* by an overwhelming majority *porque se presta* so well to combinations *con inglés.*

Follow these examples:

> *Eso está* **messed up.**
>
> *Estás* **harshing my mellow.**
>
> *Estoy* **down with that.**
>
> *Estamos* **crazy busy.**
>
> *Estuvimos* **brainwashed.**

Pretty easy, huh? Pretty fun, too. *Estarás* amazed at how often this rule comes into play. *Bueno,* I think *que ya deben estar* ready to try it out yourselves.

SPANGLISH RULE #193

Kick off your switch *con un* quote.

Anything *"entre comillas"* is automatically set apart from whatever *acabas de decir.* Which is an extremely convenient juncture *para hacer el brinquito* to another language.

If you're speaking Spanish but relating *una conversación* conducted originally *en inglés*, simply switch back to English for what you are quoting. And vice versa. This way you don't have to translate, *y capturarás el sabor original de lo que se dijo.* It's the most direct way of conveying a bit of dialogue as it was recorded by your memory.

Quote switches, *de hecho*, are often prompted by emotional triggers linked to memory. *Si estás hablando de* your *mami* or *papi, y tienes un* relationship *con* that parent *en español*, chances are *que tu* brain will shift *automáticamente* into *Telemundo* mode. It's a very natural thing, *así que* go with it.

And *una vez que hagas el* switch, feel free to keep *switcheando* between languages within the quoted dialogue (*siguiendo siempre* general usage and abusage guidelines).

Here's how it's done:

So I told her straight out, *"¿Sabes qué? Déjate de ser* such a backstabber."

Pues, eso le dije: "Let's just be friends, *pero con* benefits."

Like they say, *"Tienes que* use it or *si no* you lose it."

His lame excuse was, *"No te pude llamar porque mi teléfono se cayó en el* toilet."

Y él me dice, "Terrorism? That's the least of my worries. *Mírate este* haircut."

Pero me dije a mí misma, "It sounds pretty iffy. *Yo no voy a invertir tanto dinero en ningún* ostrich farm."

My father would always say, *"Un clavo saca a otro clavo."* And I always thought, "Yeah, but, *un clavo* can also push another *clavo* in deeper."

Entonces me dijo, "No way I'm going to the circus *porque me paniquean los* clowns."

Never miss an opportunity to quote someone else or something you yourself may have said or thought, *porque las citas son un* gateway to Spanglish. Remember, whether you are speaking in English or Spanish, when quoting something originally expressed in the alternate *idioma,* switch back to that *idioma* to kick off that quote. Why? *Porque* because it works.

Y puedes quote me on that.

SPANGLISH RULE #75

Stay reflexive and objective.

One of the most Spanglish of all the Spanglish reflexes is to switch *entre idiomas,* specifically from English into Spanish, *utilizando los* reflexive pronouns. And, *ahora que* I reflect on it, *esto mismo sucede* with object pronouns too. *Debería tener mucho que ver* with the fact *de que* all these little pronoun words sound the same. *Palabritas* like *se, te, me, le,* etc. At least *así me parece.*

Si necesitan review what the hell reflexive and objective pronouns are, *pues tómense un momento* and *googléenlo.* That's what the Internet is for. *Y cuan-*

do terminen su online *repaso,* we'll take a look at *cómo se emplea este* little understood principle *del* Spanglish.

OK. *¿Listos?* Here we go.

> *Ave María,* breakfast in bed. *Te pasaste con los* Egg McMuffins.
>
> *Es que* he's so gullible, *se dejó llevar,* hook, line, and sinker.
>
> Careful, that dog *le muerde a* everybody.
>
> Spending *tres horas comprando* hiking shoes for a one-hour hike, *me parece una locura.*
>
> *El* taxi driver *nos quizo cobrar* too much. *Le dije,* "Are you crazy? *Mejor caminamos.*"
>
> After he threw up, *se quiso montar en el* roller coaster *otra vez.*

By the way, we have a job opening at the Santiago Spanglish Institute for World Peace for anyone who understands why this works. *Favor de emailear* your resume to: thinktank@porquebecause.com.

Pero the fact is *que* not only does it work, native Spanglish *hablantes* do it all the time. And if you want to sound like a native, *lo tienes que hacer también.*

SPANGLISH RULE #40

The *"era to"* is bilingual glue.

Spanglish is full of weird little linkages *que surgen* naturally over and over again. One of my favorite is the "*era* to" combo. Pronounced *como si fuera* one word, "*era* to" makes for a very sturdy *empate* between *el inglés y el español.* Of course, the word "*era*" means "was," as it is the past tense of the Spanish verb "*ser*," meaning "to be."

What's interesting is the uniqueness of this combo's overlapping grammatical structure. *Efectivamente,* it reconciles the component *idiomas* at the switch point, *casi a las malas* for a forced fit.

Take a look at these *ejemplos* and you'll see what I mean.

Lo que necesitaba era to don't say nothing.

Lo que hizo era to make it worse.

El propósito era to not spend *su vida entera* slaving away *en un* cubicle.

Lo que soñaba era to make it big. *Bueno, por lo menos,* not so small.

Tal vez the fancy dinner *era* to make believe *que no estaba tan* broke.

The only reason he pretended to like her poetry *era* to *llevársela a la cama.*

Now, *por raro que suene,* it works great, right? *Debido a ciertas idiosincrasias, se emplea* almost always *para hacer el* switching from Spanish to English. But it is used *para switcheos* in the other direction, *de vez en cuando.*

El motivo for my adding it to *los* rules here *era* to *asegurar* it was in your bag of *trucos.*

SPANGLISH RULE #312

Raise your eyebrows when you say *"¡Imagínate!"*

Liberal, imaginative use of the word *"imagínate,"* which means "imagine" in Spanish, is a staple of Spanglish conversations. It's also one of the most popular switch words between English and Spanish.

Utilízalo to set up or tag statements *de los cuales* one is supposed to be even *un poquitito* shocked. It tips off listeners to the fact *de que* you think *lo que estás diciendo* is alarming or *escandaloso* and that you expect *que ellos estén de acuerdo*. For instance: "I left the stove on, *imagínate*." Or, "*Imagínate*, he puts ketchup on his *tostones*."

I also highly recommended that you truncate the expression, to simply *"¡'Magínate!"* This really helps punctuate any given sentence. Either way, using *imagínate* or *'magínate* in Spanish works beautifully for emphasis. *Sin embargo*, note what happens *cuando lo hacemos* in reverse:

Se me pudiera haber quemado la casa. **Imagine.**

Yeah, I know. It kind of peters off there at the end. *En vez de* kicking up *el tono emocional*, when you switch out of Spanish and into English, *para decir* "Imagine," it's sort of an anticlimactic transition in pitch. *¿Verdad que sí?*

There is something colloquial about *"imagínate"* in Spanish that is exclamatory in and of itself, *subrayando* the shocking nature of whatever statement it's being attached to. I bet you *que tiene algo que ver* with the accent over the letter "i" *cuando se dice en español.*

A more equivalent translation for "*Imagínate*" into English *más bien sería* "Can you imagine?" Which, even when said emphatically, still leans more toward a question than an exclamation. *Además en español,* the one word (or less) versions are more common, debunking *el mito de que* English is always shorter and more efficient. *¡'Maginate!*

Facial expression is a very important component in the proper Spanglish use of this word as an interjection. Go for a wide-eyed delivery, remembering to always raise your eyebrows (or unibrow *si estás* sporting *cejas a lo* Frida). Do this *aunque estés hablando por teléfono* because *la persona* on the other end will be able to tell.

SPANGLISH RULE NUMBER #1

All Spanglish rules are subject to change.

Porque because.

SPANGLISH RULE NUMBER #99

Count on "*que*" as switch word *número uno.*

La verdad del caso es que there would be no Spanglish without the word "*que.*"

"*¿Qué qué?*" you say. Yes, that's right. *No estoy* exaggerating. It's absolutely critical.

It facilitates *todo tipo de* switches between English and Spanish. *Única en su versatilidad*, this all-purpose *palabra* functions in an amazing number of ways, including as a conjunction, as a relative pronoun, as an adjective, as an adverb, and as an interrogative.

And *además* it's also the second half of the word *porque*.

Which is the reason *por qué* the word *"que" se escucha tanto* in Spanglish. People of the *habla* have come to rely on it as the gaffer's tape of their *idioma*, because it's so handy.

Here's a bunch of examples *que demuestran la variedad de maneras en que* this mother of all switch words *hace que el* Spanglish *sea posible.* I won't break down exactly *qué* part of speech the *"que"* functions as in each case. *Pero por favor* feel free to do that yourself *como* homework.

> ***Después que* we elect them, *hay que* keep them honest.**
>
> ***¡Ay qué* cute!** *¡Adoro los* **puggles!**
>
> ***¿Qué* what?* That bastard *se pegó la loto? ¡Qué suerte tiene ese sonamabiche!***
>
> **What happened was *que nadie le dijo que* she was on the rebound.**
>
> ***¿Sabes qué?* You're fired!**

So you see, *es que* the word *"que"* is really indispensable. *Ninguna otra palabra* gets you as easily in and out of either language. *Así que* make it your default switch word *y verás que* you can't go wrong.

Well, that's more Spanglish rules than ever compiled anywhere by anybody yet! *Y por más incompleta que sea la lista en el momento*, it's more than enough to get you through the rest of the book. Next, *se discutirán estrategias de como* to get into the habit of applying *los* rules.

TOP TEN MYTHS ABOUT LATINOS

1. LATINOS ARE NOT PUNCTUALITY CHALLENGED. WE'RE FASHIONABLY *TARDE.*

2. LATINOS ARE NOT AGAINST ASSIMILATION. IF YOU WANT TO ASSIMILATE INTO OUR CULTURE, *PUES BIENVENIDO.*

3. LATINOS ARE NOT ALWAYS FESTIVE. WE JUST NEVER LET BEING DEPRESSED GET IN THE WAY OF A GOOD TIME.

4. LATINA WOMEN DO NOT DRESS ANY MORE PROVOCATIVELY THAN OTHER WOMEN. THEY JUST LOOK MORE PROVOCATIVE NO MATTER WHAT THEY'RE WEARING.

5. BEING LATINO DOESN'T AUTOMATICALLY MEAN YOU CAN DANCE SALSA, OR MERENGUE, OR BACHATA OR TANGO. BUT IT DOES IMPROVE YOUR ODDS SIGNIFICANTLY.

6. LATINOS ARE NOT ALL MEXICAN. EXCEPT IN CALIFORNIA.

7. LATINOS DON'T COME HERE TO DO THE JOBS NO ONE ELSE WANTS TO DO. THEY COME TO DO THE JOBS EVEN THEY DON'T WANT TO DO. *PORQUE* THEY NEED THE *DINERO.*

8. A *CHALUPA* IS NOT AN EDIBLE CHIHUAHUA.

9. MOST LATINOS DO NOT PREFER TO SPEAK SPANISH. WE PREFER TO SPEAK THE MORE BEAUTIFUL LANGUAGE, WHICH HAPPENS TO BE SPANISH.

10. LATINOS DON'T HAVE ANYTHING AGAINST BLACKS. BUT THEY WOULD LIKE A FAIR SHOT ON "SHOWTIME AT THE APOLLO."

4

THE SEVEN MALAS COSTUMBRES

OF HIGHLY EFFECTIVE SPANGLISH
HABLANTES

I'll have another Jägermeister, *por favor.*

—something you'll never hear a Latino say

You gotta get in the habit of Spanglish *si quieres lograr ser* any good at it. But good habits will get you nowhere. *Para poder alcanzar* maximum Spanglishicity *lo más rápido posible*, you need to adopt the very worst habits *inmediatamente.*

Dado que hay so many *malas costumbres* that the best Spanglish speakers *están* in the habit of, *pensé que sería muy* useful to present you *con las cuales* my research has proven to give *los mejores resultados.* Adopt them faithfully, *y de este modo* you will soon know the sweet blasphemy *que tanto disfrutamos nosotros* of the *habla.*

Simple, *pero poderosas,* each of these *malas costumbres* will significantly improve your Spanglish proficiency *a largo plazo.* Unlike good habits, *verán cómo de fácil* they become second nature. *Es más*, you may be unconsciously practicing *algunas de ellas* already. *En dado caso*, learning them formally *y aplicándolas* deliberately, *asegurará que podrás* maximize your Spanglish potential.

So, let's run them down first. *Y luego las explico.*

> *Mala Costumbre* #1: To Thine Own Self Speak Spanglish
>
> *Mala Costumbre* #2: Don't Sweat *La Gramática*
>
> *Mala Costumbre* #3: Fake It *Hasta Que* You Make It
>
> *Mala Costumbre* #4: Get Over *El* Imaginary Lingual Divide
>
> *Mala Costumbre* #5: Catch the *Mariposa* Effect
>
> *Mala Costumbre* #6: Practice Random Acts of Spanglish
>
> *Mala Costumbre* #7: Set Your Tongue to Telemundo

To Thine Own Self Speak Spanglish

Admit it, you talk to yourself. *¡Yo también!* It's one of the *seven malas costumbres* of highly effective Spanglish-*hablantes*. So start as soon as you get up in the morning. "Mirror, mirror on the wall, who's *el* most *chulísimo papi* of them all?" I usually whisper it, *porque* because one time my girlfriend overheard me, and the answer came back: "*¡Chayanne!*"

Pero anyway, starting out your day first thing with a little self-*habla* will really get your Spanglish juices going. *Te pone* ready internally *para enfrentar al mundo.* Keep up the running commentary *mientras que* you mutter to yourself about *esto y lo otro.*

For example:

About the dreary day *que te espera* outside: "*Ay el* weather *está* nasty. *Y yo con ganas de acostarme y no hacer nada.* Oh my god, *¡Qué frío!*"

About the neighbor *quien tiene el descaro de caminar sus perros* in your yard: "*Híjole, pero qué* low life."

About the "*¡Basta ya!*" breaking point in your love life: "*Estoy harta de tener una relación de* long distance. That's it, *esto no puede seguir así.*"

About your Halloween costume: "I know! This year *me disfrazo de* Ugly Betty. *Con los* braces *y todo.*"

About getting hungry: "Oh, there go *mis tripitas* again. *Me están dando los* munchies."

Talking to yourself is a language habit worth its *peso en oro* for any serious student and practitioner of the *habla.* And *no te preocupes* about doing it in public, either. Just pretend *que estás hablando en tu* cell phone, *para que nadie piense que estás medio* crazy.

Don't Sweat *La Gramática*

As every effective Spanglish *hablante* knows, the only syntactical *pecado* is to play it safe. Unofficial rules of Spanglish exist, *como ya vieron en el último* chapter, "*Los* Rules of Engagement." *Pero,* for now, while there are still no official dos and don'ts, don't let anything cramp *tu estilo.* Make it a habit to improvise the grammar of both *idiomas* and never doubt yourself while you're doing it. Better said: *Nunca dudes,* dude. Just *hazlo!*

Siempre keep in mind *que el* Spanglish *es demasiado difícil* to mess up any more than it already is messed up—by definition. In other words, *no lo vas a chingar más de la cuenta,* so why feel guilty? If there's such a thing as a grammatical envelope, I say, "*¡Púshalo, mijo!*"

Fake It *Hasta Que* You Make It

Sounds wacky, *pero funciona.* Faking it, *estar* pretending, *puede ser un* powerful tool *para* self-*mejoramiento.* Behave *como si ya fueras un* Spanglish speaker, and you become the Spanglish speaker *que tanto deseas ser.*

Eventually, your Spanglish alter ego *se apoderará de tu* personality. *La idea* is to fake it so good *que* you fake yourself into thinking *que* you're not faking it, *y entonces* you don't have to fake it anymore. *Gotita a gotita, pasito a pasito,* your new Spanglish behaviors *crean tu nueva* Spanglish identity.

Live the part, *como si fueras un* actor preparing for a Spanglish role. If it helps, get a tattoo *que dice "¡Porque* because!" some place embarrassing on your body.

Por último, if by any chance you never make it, *pues ni modo.* Simply *sigue* faking it.

Get Over *El* Imaginary Lingual Divide

One of the greatest *obstáculos* to effective Spanglish is imaginary. There is no actual barrier, wall, or division between English and Spanish. *No hay nada* preventing you from *estar switcheando* back and forth. You don't have to apply for a visa. You don't have to go through security. You don't have to take off your shoes for anybody.

¡El único hurdle *está en tu cabeza! Pero* everybody *se pone* all bent out of shape about it. As if they didn't have *permiso* or it was against some moral law. If they're speaking in Spanish *y de repente se brincan al inglés* without meaning to, *quieren* report themselves to the language police, *de lo* guilty *que se sienten.*

Get over it. *Y pa'lante con el* Spanglish!

Catch the *Mariposa* Effect

If a butterfly can change the weather patterns by fluttering its wings, as stated in a scientific theory known as the "Butterfly Effect," *claro que* Spanglish can have *un semejante impacto* global.

I call my theory the "*Porque* Because" effect. By flapping your gums to speak Spanglish, *en consecuencia y debido a ello*, you can spark a Spanglish conversation *en otra esquinita del planeta* unleashing *una tormenta de* Spanglish. Via the interconnectivity of humanity's collective lingual consciousness, *cada palabra de* Spanglish *que se hable* yields a ripple effect *por todo el sistema*.

Ahora, exactly how this works, *ni tengo idea*. *Pero*, think of yourself as a bilingual *mariposa* fluttering about in the Spanglish matrix, your gossamer *alas* (one representing English, one Spanish) powered by and perpetuating reverberations of the *habla*. Every time *que flapeamos nuestros* lips it makes a difference.

The cumulative result is a Spanglish metamorphosis of the world. *Así que* catch *el efecto* butterfly. Make a conscious habit of it. And be a catalyst for *cambio*.

Practice Random Acts of Spanglish

Sprinkle Spanglish wherever you go. Be creative and incorrigible about it.

Slap a bumper sticker on a stranger's car that says, "Honk, *si eres indocumentado*." Put a sign on the Brooklyn Bridge *que diga*: "*Se Vende*. $5 *Pesos*. Or Best Offer."

Call your local representative and say, "*Mira, estoy* sick and tired *de lo que está pasando* in this damn country. *What* are you doing, taking *unas vacaciones cuando* there's so much work to do? *Le digo,* I'm not gonna stand for it anymore, and I can't wait to vote against you—as soon as I become a citizen!" From now on, always make a Spanglish impression when you make an exit. Never just say "Good-bye" or "*Adiós*." Look into people's eyes and say, "May the *habla* be with you."

Set Your Tongue to Telemundo

The word "Telemundo" has become slang among non-Latinos for all things Spanish. This goes back to non-Latinos lumping every Spanish-language channel on TV, *por falta de conocimiento y algo de ignorancia voluntaria,* under the same brand name. It doesn't matter if it's Univisión, TV Azteca, Galavisión, Telefutura, or HBO Latino—it's all Telemundo as far as they're concerned.

Moreover, *este* meaning *ha sido* extended further *y de una forma graciosísima.* One day I started speaking Spanish (involuntarily, *¡sin saberlo!*) to a non–Spanish speaker *quien se freakeó* and cut me off immediately by saying, "Whoa, whoa, whoa! Don't get all Telemundo on me!"

Estuve blown away *cuando* I first heard this usage.

Cargada de connotaciones culturales, this catchall *palabra,* transformed by *su nuevo contexto,* leaps beyond a mere *sinónimo* for all Spanish TV. It's become shorthand for the parallel world occasionally glimpsed by non-Latinos, *mientras hacen el* channel surfing *por todos esos* over-the-top Latino networks— shamelessly *exagerados,* impossibly *calientes,* inexplicably *emocionales,* and preposterously *apasionados.*

The word, *hoy en día,* refers to this other reality *en español,* to a brave new *mundo,* a Telemundo.

Bueno, there you have them. *Estudien y apliquen los principios* until these seven bad habits, *las malas costumbres más deseables,* become automatic reflexes. Combined and faithfully adhered to, *estas poderosas llaves del éxito* will help anyone *alcanzar destacados niveles de* Spanglish.

So keep *hablando el* talk, *caminando el* walk, and remember, *no hay* Spanglish *que por bien no venga.*

TOP TEN SPANGLISH PROVERBS

1. IF AT FIRST *FRACASAS,* TRY, TRY *OTRA VEZ.*

2. LIFE *ES UNA JODIENDA,* AND THEN YOU DIE.

3. TO *OPRIMA EL DOS* OR NOT TO *OPRIMA EL DOS.* THAT IS *LA PREGUNTA.*

4. *HAY QUE* THINK OUTSIDE THE TACO.

5. FAKE IT *HASTA QUE* YOU MAKE IT.

6. *NO SE PUEDE TROSTEAR A* NOBODY.

7. SOMETIMES YOU HAVE TO TAKE ONE FOR *EL TEAMO.*

8. *TIENES QUE* USE IT OR *SI NO* YOU LOSE IT.

9. *LO QUE* GOES AROUND *VIENE PA'TRÁS* AROUND.

10. *NUNCA DEBES* JUDGE *A NADIE, HASTA QUE* YOU'VE WALKED AROUND *EN SUS CHANCLAS.*

5

SPANGLISH

A LO GRINGO

**"Just admit it, Ramos. Your people are planning
a *reconquista*. Aren't they?"**

—Lou "El Gordo" Dobbs of CNN interviewing Jorge Ramos of Univisión

Who Are You Calling a Gringo?

I can understand how some people might take exception to the term
"gringo." I got called gringo once *y casi* burst into tears. It happened in
Venezuela and I was stunned. There I was, sporting the best tan of my life,
bien pero bien prietito, carrying an autographed copy of Gabriel García
Márquez's "*Cien Años de Soledad*," whistling "*Pedro Navaja*," and wearing my
favorite plantain-stained *guayabera*.

How could someone call me, of all people, that horribly derogatory
word when I was radiating such a pan-Latino vibe? I said, "Just one cotton
pickin' *momentito*! Who are you *llamando un* gringo?"

The woman serving me at the *arepa* stand, who had just cheerfully insulted me, explained that, as far as she was concerned, anyone not from Venezuela was a gringo.

What about Antonio Banderas? I asked, testing her definition. "*Gringo*," she said. What about Shakira? "*Gringa*," she said again, holding firm. Sammy Sosa? "*Gringo*." Gael García Bernal? "*Gringo, por más* cute *que sea*." Salma Hayek? "*Gringa*." Benicio del Toro? "*Gringo, punto, lo siento*."

Well, at least I was in good company, I thought.

Turns out, all across Latin America this word is used in the broadest sense to mean any outsider or foreigner. Of course, it also commonly denotes a straight-up generic American with a certain lack of pigmentation, from the United States, as opposed to someone Latino or Spanish-speaking.

Sometimes it's employed as a term of endearment, not unlike *wetback*, *dago*, and *spic*. A lot of Americans don't appreciate being called *gringo*, but admit they prefer it to big fat *turista*.

Nobody complains, however, in situations where the designation confers clear advantages. As in: "Now pre-boarding all gringos."

In Argentina they call Italians gringos. Nazis, they call Brazilians. In Spain, they don't use gringo too much, but I have one Spanish friend who calls all Mexicans gringos. In Mexico, *gringo* can mean anyone from the United States, regardless of ethnicity, or anyone blonde (natural or dyed!), tall, fair-skinned with blue eyes (a.k.a. *güero*), regardless of nationality.

Not Easy Being Green

Not only are there endless shades of connotation, but theories on the origin of the term *gringo* abound. Oh, boy, where to begin?

Some say *gringo* derives from the green uniforms worn by United States soldiers during the Mexican American War. Supposedly, Mexicans who didn't particularly approve of the invasion got in the habit of shouting "Green Go!" as a reflex reaction to all things American, especially their faces.

Less credible sources swear the term traces back to popular Mexican lore, which attributes American victory in the war to a special-forces battalion of Irish leprechauns in the U.S. army.

Although never actually seen by any Mexicans, it is said the tiny mercenaries were often heard singing: "We're green, and we'll go wherever we must. We'll fight you with magic, just don't step on us. We're green and we go to war for the yanks. They pay us with gold, it's better than thanks. Hi ho, hi ho, green go, green go, green go . . . "

More than one online dictionary suggests the term *gringo* may derive from *griego*, the Spanish word for "Greek." It was extended to mean anything foreign, as a carry-over from the phrase, "Sounds like Greek to me." But I am more inclined to believe in the leprechaun story.

Remembering the Alamo

My own research, however, has just uncovered evidence of another possibility. Previously unknown, Mexican general Antonio de Padua María Severino López de Santa Anna and American hero Davy Crockett, king of the wild frontier, American statesman, and eventual Disney character, maintained a friendly correspondence for years.

In the days leading up to the Battle of the Alamo, Santa Anna expressed his disgust with the American presence there. Crockett dashed off a short letter to his *amigo* counseling restraint: "You'll just have to grin and bear it." Santa Anna replied, curtly: "I'll grin, when they go."

The exchange was probably leaked intentionally and went viral.

No Offense?

Should anyone be offended by being called gringo?

It isn't necessarily affectionate or pejorative these days. It depends on your personal definition and perception of the intended meaning. You can usually tell from inflection, tone of voice, and context whether *se dice con cariño* or not.

Some gringos actually love being called gringo. I mean, I've never heard of a gringo pride parade. But still many gringos *se identifican como tal* with tremendous gringo pride. A former journalism colleague of mine who moonlighted as a *merengue* percussionist in Old San Juan even went by the stage name of *El Gringo Sabroso*.

I'd say the general consensus is that being called gringo is no cause for offense—except when preceded by words like "*maldito*," or "*pinche*," or "*foking*."

I know there are a lot of gringos reading this book right now. In fact, this is probably the first chapter you opened up to, just to see what I had to say about your particular Spanglish ways. Do I approve? Do I feel your contributions to the *habla* will benefit humankind in the long run? Do I think you should stop embarrassing yourselves?

Well, and I think I speak for a lot of Latinos when I say this: At least you're not dancing the Macarena anymore. Seriously, you gringos do some pretty amazing things with Spanglish and have gone above and beyond the call of linguistic blasphemy to develop your own proprietary blend.

One of the key aspects (advantages even) of gringo Spanglish is that you get to speak Spanish wrong on purpose! No attempt to get it right is ever necessary. Not surprisingly, "No *problemo*" is the undisputed king of gringo Spanglish phrases. In fact, it's no *surprise-o*. Spanish and English share so many practically identical words that many non-Spanish speakers take it for granted that *hablaring español* must be *no problemo* at all.

Gringa *de Pura Cepa*

For the record, just because you have exhibited an ATM-level of proficiency in Spanish does not mean you're fluent. Don't expect to blend in and converse with the natives south of the border, or the day laborers standing outside Home Depot, simply because you conduct a financial transaction *en español* on a goof and are able to successfully *retirar* some *dinero* from your *cuenta corriente* by swiping *el* card-*o* through *la* machine-*o*.

Pero claro, overconfidence in rudimentary Spanish is a dead giveaway trait of the gringo Spanglish *hablante*.

My friend Tamara, who is so *gringa* she doesn't even know how *gringa* she is, just traveled to Latin America certain that she was fluent enough to get by. After seven years of high-school Spanish, she knew exactly two sentences: "*No me toques*" and "*Más cerveza por favor.*" Of course, bar-hopping her way through Costa Rica, she realized the more she said "*más cerveza*," the more she had to fend off overly friendly drinking buddies with, "¡*No me toques!*"

She would often drunk-dial me from Central America, asking me to translate Spanish pickup lines. "Bill, you gotta help me out on this one. I think he just told me I'm like a *lomo*, a piece of meat, and that he wants to be a fried egg and lie next to me."

Anyway, back here in *los* United States, the Spanglish homeland, gringos are nevertheless equal partners in the Spanglish revolution. We couldn't do it without you. Precisely because of your limited Spanish, you come up with some doozies that would never even occur to us. So please accept my personal heartfelt *grassy-ass*.

But I should make clear that for the purposes of this *muy importante* discussion, *gringo* does not necessarily mean *blanquito*.

Granted, the *blanquitos* are leading the gringo pack. But I live up in Harlem, on 144th Street in New York City, and my downstairs neighbor, J. T., a tireless African American entrepreneur whose parents were from Barbados and Atlanta, never misses the Puerto Rican Day Parade.

He's out there every year, trying to make a buck and unload his inventory, shouting, "Get your flag-o! *Uno* dollar! Show your *boricua* pride-o! *Uno* dollar! Get your flag-o! *¡Ay caramba!*, that's what I'm talkin' 'bout. Just *uno* dollar . . ."

Guac Around the Clock

A lot of Spanish enters the gringo realm via the mouth before it ever comes out as Spanglish. Basically, if a Spanish menu item tastes good enough, it gets fast-tracked into standard American English. And once "the whole *enchilada*" replaced "the whole kit and caboodle" as an idiom, there was really no turning *pa'trás*. By the way, have you ever tasted a kit and caboodle? Neither have I. But them *enchiladas* are damn tasty.

Lately, a lot of gringos are going around saying "*guac*," instead of "*guacamole*" as a standard abbreviation. "That was good *guac*." "Wanna get some *guac?*" "Awesome *guac*, dude." "I don't think that's gonna be enough *guac* for everybody." "We're gonna *guac guac guac* till broad daylight. We're gonna *guaca guaca guaca* around the clock tonight . . . "

Very creative stuff. *¿No les parece?*

I'm a big fan of Anglocentric expressions that take Spanglish to the next level. Like this one, *posteado en un* blog the other day: "After Spanish class, we went out *bailamos*-ing to salsa tunes!" I laughed so much when I read it because it actually made sense to me. And I am willing to bet that this *gringo loco* conjugation of the verb *bailar* derives from overexposure to that Enrique Iglesias song.

Loco for *Loco*

Speaking of *loco*, I'm always amused by just how *loco* gringos happen to be about the word *loco*. I think it's because they can only understand typical Latino behavior as some sort of brain malfunction.

I mean, why are we Latinos so loud, touchy-feely, emotional, and festive? Why do we have astrology readings on our hard news programs? How is it we're never on time but always on beat?

This is obviously a more crazy kind of crazy. Not just crazy. *¡Loco!* And so gringos have adopted the word to express an exaggerated type of hotheaded nutcase or insanely ludicrous situation.

What's *loco* is that *loco* also happens to be the word most frequently used by Latinos to describe gringos. "*Ahí llegó el gringo loco.*" "*Pero y ese gringo loco, ¿qué se trae?*" "*Oye, ese gringo loco, sí que está loco.*" "*No le hagas caso al gringo loco ése.*" "*Siempre tiene que haber un gringo loco.*"

At least we appreciate one another's questionable mental faculties.

"O" My!

Loco or not, gringos are crazy busy on their end of the Spanglish spectrum pushing the envelope-*o*. I am in awe of how they can convert any English word into "close-enough Spanish" simply by tacking a vowel (mostly "*o*") at the end.

"Close enough Spanish" is very popular in the anglosphere. You don't want to give the impression that you actually know another language. Your friends and neighbors might suspect you of being unpatriotic.

Sure, there are gringos who throw caution to the wind and make the effort to learn proper Spanglish. It's usually those insufferable multi-cultier-than-thou gringos who believe they were Latino in another life.

Those Che-Guevara-T-shirt-wearing-Neruda-reciting-salsa-on-2-dancing-Lou-Dobbs-hating-Chiapas-revolution-sympathizing-*nuevo*-Latino-cuisine-eating-*Feliz-Navidad*-singing-*palabra-del-día*-subscribing-English-only-protesting-*la-raza*-loving-*oprima-el dos*-pushing-Telemundo-watching-Frida-Kahlo-unibrow-admiring-*santería*-dabbling-Cuba-embargo-violating-Christopher-Columbus-blaming-immigration-amnesty-wanting-*Virgen-de-Guadalupe*-praying-*mojito*-sipping-gringos tend to speak the flashier Spanglish, sometimes well enough to go *mano a mano* with Latinos.

But if you want to sound like an authentic gringo, even if you know how to say something correctly when you switch into Spanish—don't. *A nadie le gusta un* show-off.

Despite its English-dominant nature and comparatively shallow pool of Spanish vocabulary, everyday gringo Spanglish still affords plenty of range. After getting up to speed over the last century or so, it has become extremely versatile and can be used for infinite reasons.

To address superheroes: "Holy *frijoles,* Batman!"

To be hospitable: "Welcome. *Mi cama es tu cama.*"

To ask for directions: "How do I get to *el* town-*o*?"

To complain about your hotel: "*El* stupid vending machine-*o* was out of *la* order and I couldn't get *el* snack-*o*."

To make political statements: "Those non-transfat-*istas* are full of *crapola.*"

To tell off another surfer: "*Chinga tu madre,* dude."

To comment on Latino celebrities: "I heard Marc Anthony won't even let her do photo shoots by herself. He's very *machismo.*"

To express teenage indifference: "*Que*-ever . . . "

To confirm the plumbing emergency is under control: "José is in the bathroom right now, *arreglar*-ing the toilet situation."

To indicate musical preferences: "Vincente Fernández is OK. But I'm much more in simpatico with Willie Nelson."

To give a hilarious comedian props: "Oh my God, Bill, you rocked *la casa!*"

However, because of some mysterious linguistic idiosyncrasy, gringo Spanglish seems to be especially useful for expressing negation, exasperation, or dismissal:

"No way, *José!*"

"Zip, zilch, *nada!*"

"*Hasta la vista,* baby!"

"I can't take it anymore. *¡No más!*"

"It's over, *finito, el* done-*o*!"

"*¡Basta!* Before I bust a cap in your *culo!*"

Spanish and pseudo-Spanish words and phrases pour constantly from the mouths of monolinguals in this country who don't really know Spanish per se. In fact, gringos enjoy a certain advantage as Spanglish speakers over Latinos. Nobody expects them to get Spanish right, so they can be a lot less inhibited about experimenting. Whereas if a Latino screws up the Spanish, *¡ay, qué vergüenza!* You feel you're going to get disowned by your family or banned from watching "*Sábado Gigante*" or have your tortilla privileges taken away.

Pero anyway, Spanglish thrives in Gringolandia. It's so embedded in the mainstream *que la gran mayoría de los gringos andan* blissfully unaware of it *hasta que* you bring it to their attention.

Last night I performed at the Hermosa Comedy and Magic Club, one of the best clubs in the country, just south of Los Angeles on a lovely little strip of *playa* called Hermosa Beach. The crowd was unusually diverse for Hermosa Beach, meaning every shade of gringo was well represented. And nobody in the audience knew that *hermosa* is a Spanish word meaning "beautiful."

¡Imagínate! They live in a Spanglish town *sin saberlo!*

I remember I got lost on my way to play at this club for the very first time. I pulled over to ask someone for directions. The guy didn't seem to get me when I asked in English, so I asked in Spanish how to get to *Hermosa* Beach. "*Pues, cualquiera,*" he said. "They're all beautiful."

TOP TEN TIPS FOR SPEAKING SPANGLISH LIKE A GRINGO

1. REFRAIN FROM SPANISH CONJUGATION OF ANY KIND.

2. ADD SPANISH ARTICLES TO ENGLISH WORDS, BEING CAREFUL TO SCREW UP GENDER AND NUMBER AGREEMENT.

3. NEVER MISS A CHANCE TO MISPRONOUNCE A SPANISH WORD SO BADLY THAT IT'S NO LONGER RECOGNIZABLE TO A SPANISH-SPEAKING PERSON.

4. TRILL YOUR R'S AS IF COUGHING UP A FUR BALL.

5. ALWAYS MAINTAIN THE FOLLOWING ATTITUDE: "WHAT DO YOU EXPECT? I'M A GRINGO."

6. EMPLOY LIBERAL, SOCIALLY AWKWARD USE OF THE WORD *PENDEJO*.

7. HYPERASPIRATE YOUR "H" SOUNDS SO THAT YOU SEEM TO BE GASPING FOR OXYGEN WHEN YOU SAY WORDS LIKE *CUANTO* (KUWHHHAANTOHHH), *POQUITO* (POHHHKHHHEETOHHH), AND *ESCUELA* (ESKUWHHHAYLAHHH).

8. REMEMBER WHAT THEY TOLD YOU IN SPANISH CLASS ABOUT HOW THE DOUBLE "L" (EL) SOUND IS PRONOUNCED LIKE A "Y" IN ENGLISH? WELL, FORGET THAT AND JUST PRONOUNCE IT LIKE A LAW-ABIDING AMERICAN CITIZEN.

9. THOSE SQUIGGLY LINES HOVERING OVER SOME "N'S" IN WRITTEN SPANISH? PRETEND YOU NEVER SAW THEM.

10. WHEN ALL ELSE FAILS, THROW IN AN "¡AY CARAMBA!"

6

HOME SWEET
SPANGLISH HOME

The Spanglish genie, *se ha escapado de la botella.*

—*"Los* Trends *Más* Cool Magazine*"*

Long before *se puso de moda*, I grew up in a house where *hasta los perros* were fluent in Spanglish. Our dogs understood and responded to a mega mix of both languages. And we would automatically translate their barks back into Spanglish as well. For instance, our Puerto Rican attack poodle, Ciclone, *ladraba*, "Arf! Arf!" And I would explain on his behalf, "*Mira, que* he wants a milkbone."

I'm sure most of you can relate, right? Spanglish *en casa* is pretty standard these days. *¿Qué* what? You don't have Spanglish at home yet? *Pues, estás* crazy *atrasado*. You might as well still be on dial-up, *por Dios!*

In fact, think of Spanglish as *un* broadband *lingüístico*, providing modern Latinos (and those who love them) with the capacity, range, and speed necessary for seamless, shameless switching between English and Spanish. *Hasta se podría decir que* it's becoming impossible to conduct our *vidas cotidianas* without it. At least *en este país.*

In case you missed it, the United States rose to first place in Spanglish penetration among countries surveyed recently by the Santiago Spanglish Institute for World Peace. A report titled "*¿Qué esperas*, bro?" identified the primary factors fomenting the trend here as immigration, intermarriage, and Dora the Explorer.

Although the number of households converting to Spanglish is slower in some northern states, *como* Montana *y* Wyoming, *donde* gringo resistance is formidable, growth of the *habla* shows no signs of reaching a saturated plateau.

Give Us Our Daily Spanglish

Meanwhile, we of the *habla* have a lot to say *y dependemos del* Spanglish *en nuestros hogares* as the default modality in which to do so. *Por lo tanto*, every home alive with the sounds of Spanglish *ha sido* psycho-linguistically wired to accommodate the torrents of daily *habla-blah* generated by today's bilingual families.

There's no occasion, topic, context, or tone not enhanced *por este avance en comunicación interpersonal*. It suits *noticias buenas y malas* and works in crisis situations as much as *para charlar sobre las tonterías más triviales*. Any conversation on your home turf *se vuelve más interesante y divertida* when bouncing *entre idiomas*.

Here are a few examples from family members at home with Spanglish.

COMMENTING ON *EL* WEATHER:

"*¡Abre la* **window** *para que entre el* **cool,** *que estamos* **sweating** *la gota gorda* **over here!**"

ON *TU SITUACIÓN ECONÓMICA:*

"This year, *no me dieron ningún* break *en los* taxes. *Así que estoy en un* budget *bien* tight."

ABOUT *LA CASA* FIXER-UPPER *QUE* YOU
WANT TO BUY:

"Dicen que está haunted. *Pero sólo necesita un* loving care."

ON THE DAY'S GOOD NEWS:

"I finally got my period. *Pero un torrente.* I went to the bathroom today, *y de repente cayó el* Niagra Falls."

ON YOUR TOOTHACHE:

"Me tengo que hacer otro root canal. *Pero* only if they put me under. *Porque* last time *no me dieron nada* and I couldn't take it. The whole time, the dentist was like, *'¡Tate quieta! ¡Tate quieta, Ms. Flores!'* And I'm like, *'¡Tate quieto* yourself! This is not pleasant.'"

ABOUT THE SEISMIC ACTIVITY IN
THE LAUNDRY ROOM:

"I thought there was an earthquake going on. *Pero es que Natalia echó demasiada ropa* in the last load *y se desbarataba la máquina* because *de lo mucho que se estaba* shaking. So now *tenemos que llamar al* guy to fix it."

ON RAT NIGHTMARES:

"Fui a tirar la basura and I noticed one of the garbage bags on top was moving. *Me fijé* and, oh my God, *habían yo no sé cuántas ratas comiéndose los* leftovers. *¡Qué susto de madre verlas así tan grandotas y tan feas!* And after that, *no me podía dormir.* I mean, I slept *pero con puras pesadillas* that the rats were coming in *por debajo de la puerta* to get me."

ON ACCEPTANCE:

"Mijo, are you a switch-hitter, *mijo? Porque* it's OK, *mijo.* You can come out of the dugout, *mijo. Puedes decirnos la verdad.* We are still gonna love you."

ON DEATH:

"Fíjate, murió joven. She was only 97, *tú sabes.* And *todavía no se sabe* where they're going to bury her. *Eso se quedó en un* question mark. Hopefully Jersey, *porque los cementerios en Puerto Rico son* spooky scary."

ON CULTURE:

"I'm thinking *que para las Crismas, los voy a llevar a ver* 'The Nutcracker,' *pero* the Spanglish version, up at *El Teatro del Barrio.* It's called, *'El Crackeador de Cojones.'"*

ON KEEPING HOUSE:

"Ponte a recoger real good *porque esta casa está* upside down."

If you don't already have the Spanglish hookup, look at all the fun and functionality *que te estás perdiendo*. It's the best investment you'll ever make. For talking to family, visitors, and even pets in the privacy *de tu hogar*, you can't beat the always-on bandwidth that bundles *dos culturas* so beautifully into one stream of *palabras*.

The Language of *Pow Pow* for Raising Spanglish Children

Dealing with kids requires a lot of Spanglish. Especially when they get out of hand. *Según las encuestas*, most Latino parents in this country *recurren al* Spanglish to lay down the law.

Kids instinctually know that if *mami* or *papi está* flying off the handle *en español*, they must have really pushed a button *y que por ahí viene* some serious "*pow pow*." Combining *una buena regañada* with English, *el idioma del comercio*, leaves no room for doubt that you, the parent, mean business.

Timeout for *Cocotazos*

Si de timeouts *se trata*, even the most progressive parents *deben siempre* reserve the right to *repartir cocotazos*. *Cocotazos*, of course, are a standard form of *castigo* and a time-honored tradition that Latino Caribbean parents like to pass on to their children.

The name derives from *coco*, as in coconut, a metaphor for "head" or "skull," augmented by the suffix *-tazo*, which roughly translates into "upside yours." It is applied as punishment with lightning-quick speed, forcefully with one or more knuckles, by a parent to a child, and never the other way around.

A good *cocotazo* is always followed by a post-*cocotazo* phrase, such as, "*A ver si me vuelves a faltar el respeto.*" The instant improvement in behavior will last from as much as several months to as little as five seconds, depending on the degree of *malacrianza* manifest in a child.

In cases where the *malacrianza* is especially extreme because *al niño se le ha metido el diablo*, actual exorcism may be necessary. Consult with your local *botánica* about the proper method of *despojo*.

Mimi Time

Claro que el Spanglish *es* dual purpose, *en cuanto a criar a los hijos*, and can also be used in less combative situations, like when it's "time for *mimi*." As you ready little yawning *chamaquitos* for *mimi*, it is customary to reinforce cooperation by nudging their efforts along with, "*¿Ya te bañaste?* OK, *entonces* brush your teeth, *y ponte las pijamas, que te voy a leer un* bedtime story."

Y para que lo sepan, reading to children at *mimi* time *es siempre preferible* to popping in a DVD, *ya que evitará* a crying fit should there be any technical malfunctions. The other day *mi amiga* Nelly *iba a poner un* DVD *para que lo viera su hijo* Zachy. But it didn't play, causing Nelly to panic out loud about how what could have been a pleasant bonding experience was about to turn ugly. "Uh-oh, *el* DVD *de* 'Shrek' *está escratcheado* and it's not going to play . . . *Por ahí viene un* tantrum."

An experienced old-school parent, *sin embargo*, will then simply employ the most popular *pow-pow* method of not-so-last resort. Which reminds me that my favorite Spanish word is about to make the official leap into American English. The next edition of Funk and Wagnall's Unabridged Dictionary will include the word . . .

Chancla* n. /chahnk-lah/

(1) A cheap sandal that doubles as a disciplinary device in Latino households. Example: "Spare the *chancla*, spoil the child." See also, *chancletazo, fuete, tundata, and pow pow.*

(2) A code name for the "smartbomb" during the weapon's early development by the U.S. military, in reference to its swift, deadly, heat-seeking accuracy. Example: "All the *chanclas* have impacted their targets successfully, sir."

As a *chancla* survivor myself, a veteran receiver of many swift *nalgadas* and repeated target of more *cocotazos* than I can remember (probably because of *cocotazo*-related memory loss), I can testify that Spanglish and childhood go hand in hand. Yet for adults, words such as *chancla* evoke strangely fond memories. Mention it and fellow survivors laugh with recognition and offer up their own stories of how fast their mother was with the fearsome sandal.

It's a touchstone *palabra* of a common upbringing that completes its cycle only *cuando a un padre se le termina la paciencia* because their *angelitos se están portando como* little brats, thus triggering a full-on Spanglish scolding, *para que les hagan caso.*

El parenting *no es nada fácil, pero el* Spanglish *puede servir como una herramienta eficaz.* See how the *habla* works in the following child-rearing scenarios.

---

*Chancla comes from the Greek *chanklakos,* "weapon of foot," from *chankloka,* "deadly shoe," from *chankloskein,* "to punish disobedience; to teach a lesson to someone as thick-headed as a heel."

EL WIT'S END

"Se los estoy advirtiendo for the last time. *No me hagan pasar un mal rato.* Because *por mi madre se los juro,* if I have to pull this car over, everybody *se va a llevar un cocotazo!"*

POR DIOS DON'T JUST LEAVE IT THERE

"¡Búscate la pala y cepillo and clean up *este* mess *que hiciste! Que aquí tú no tienes ninguna* maid."

PERO NO SE LO DIGAS A CHILD PROTECTION

"Pues, mija, yo estoy aquí running after this monster of mine, *el* bipolar baby. I have a lot of patience, *pero él me agota mi* supply. *A veces* he drives me so crazy, *que me tomo unas cervezas* and just breast-feed him. *Te digo que* it knocks him right out."

BUT I JUST CHANGED YOU

"¡Ay fo! Hay que cambiarle los Pampers again."

NOT TO MENTION *LOS TRES MAGOS*

"Me cachó red-handed *poniendo los regalos* under the tree. Now he knows *que yo soy* Santa Claus."

CRAYOLA *FUÑONA*

"And then she, *de mala gana me contestó, y que no quería buscar* **su coloring book. And I was like, '***Ven acá,* **why you gotta be like that?'** *Porque por más* **cute** *que sea, malascrianzas no se las aguanto a nadie."*

DOUBLE TROUBLE

"Últimamente, **the twins** *me tienen* **drained out.** *Ayer,* **I swear,** *me encerraron en el* **basement,** *¡por dos horas!* **You would never know they were conspiring together, but** *es que son* **super tight** *y muy traviesos esos gemelitos."*

CUANDO ESTÁS MUY ESTRESADA, COUNT TO TEN

"Cójelo con **take it easy one** . . . *cójelo con* **take it easy two** . . . *cójelo con* **take it easy three** . . . *cójelo con* **take it easy four** . . . *cójelo con* **take it easy five** . . . *cójelo con* **take it easy six** . . . *cójelo con* **take it easy seven** . . . *cójelo con* **take it easy eight** . . . *cójelo con* **take it easy nine** . . . *cójelo con* **take it easy ten** . . ."

WHAT *LOS VECINOS* ARE SAYING ABOUT YOU

"Ay, es que ella no puede **handle** *esos* **kids.** *Están muy* **wild** *y demasiado* **spoiled. She could use** *unas clases de* **parenting."**

If You Can't Stand the Spanglish, *Salte de la Cocina*

Cuando tienes hambre, Spanglish isn't far behind. Seriously, *yo pudiera haber estado* talking nothing but English *todo el santo día,* but the second I catch a whiff of my grandmother's *arroz con gandules,* the *español* comes roaring back *como un tren zafa'o.*

Powerfully charged aromas from our comfort *comidas* set off the *"¡Qué rico!"* receptors lining the olfactory cells of our *narices,* which in turn *señalan* the *habla* cortex to go bilingual.

Physio-emotionally, *se le llama un* "code *sabroso*" response, *el cual* simultaneously activates *todas las memorias* associated *con el olor indicado.* First and foremost, childhood recollections—where the *platos típicos* of our respective *patrias* took center stage—are aroused.

Y de repente estamos respirando el aire de nuestra niñez. Even *antes del* first bite, *este aroma boreal desencadena una serie de reacciones* that puts all our systems *al máximo nivel de* Spanglish alert.

Los taste buds tingle, anticipating *enchiladas a la duranguense,* or *ropa vieja,* or *bandeja paisa,* or *locro de papas,* or *lomo de buey,* or *arepas de pescado,* or maybe *un buen asado jugoso.*

Talking with Your *Boca* Full

The exact delicacy you normally surrender to depends on your specific Latinosapien upbringing and national heritage.

I'm Puerto Rican, born in New York, or as I am known *en círculos gastronómicos,* one *mofongo*-eatin' mofo. But, the point is, our favorite *antojos* don't seem to exist except in Spanish.

And so with every mouthful, *la lengua materna se apodera.*

At the table, you weave in and out of fully bilingual conversations with family and friends, *de varias generaciones* and levels of English and Spanish fluency, as the moment dictates.

Then, *tan pronto que* you've stuffed yourself like a human *piñata, y tengas el estómago a punto de reventar*, an offer of even more food may prompt that classic, well-mannered response: "*No gracias, estoy* full."

Of course, Spanglish lends itself to any situation involving food, starting with giving a thumbs up or down on a meal:

> **"Oh my gosh, *¡esto es orgásmico!*" or "*Ese pollo sabia a* cardboard."**

Maybe you want to compliment your own *talento como* chef with a rhetorical question:

> **"*¿Qué tal estuvieron mis chilaquiles? ¿Verdad, que* they rock?"**

I recently screwed up a mission to the market for some produce and got the following scolding:

> **"*¡Pero si yo te pedí* cucumbers and you brought back zucchinis! *Qué flojo eres para hacer el* shopping."**

Now, let's say the same old cereal every morning is getting a little boring. Well, mix up the breakfast menu by suggesting:

> **"How about *en vez de cornfleys,* I make you *unos panqueques de* pistachio?"**

Pardon My *Náhuatl*

Otra cosa, you've probably noticed that as Latino culture goes mainstream, certain cuisine-related words become *muy* trendy.

Did somebody say *"chipotle"*? Yes, everybody's saying it. But are they saying it correctly? Is it: (a) chee-POHT-lay (b) chee-POHT-leh (c) chee-POtlay (d) CHEE-pot-LAY (e) chee-POTTLE? (f) CHEEP-otle?

The answer is *¿Qué sé yo?*, because it's a Náhuatl word, and since I can't even pronounce *Náhuatl*, what are the chances I'll get *chipotle* right?

In fact, rumor has it the spelling has been finagled to make a certain restaurant chain more gringo-friendly, and that it's actually supposed to be spelled *"chilpolte."* Not that you just noticed the difference, but it's there.

I can usually pronounce the name of any Latino food, even if I have no idea what it is. I had never even heard of a *quesadilla*, for example, before going to California. But I immediately figured out, from breaking down the word, that it was a squirrel (*ardilla*) covered with cheese (*queso*).

Puerto Ricans and Mexican Food

Some friends of mine took me to a Mexican restaurant once. My one friend is *puertorriqueña*. And her husband, *él es mexicano*. And *me llevaron*, one chilly California night, to one of their favorite hole in the wall joints *en las afueras de* Los Ángeles. They said it was going to be "very authentic" Mexican food, and it was, and it was great.

And on the way back, I started feeling extremely hot. You know, like really hot. *Sentí pero como un fuego*. But mostly it was my butt that was on fire. It was burning up, *de una manera que* I had never quite felt before.

I was thinking to myself, "Is it me? Is this normal? Wow, *pero esa comida* must have been very authentic." And *entonces* the husband, *quien estaba* driving, goes, "Hey, the heater in the seat is on a little too high, don't you think?"

El tipo had my seat on full blast! And there I was, *pensando que* maybe I should stick to less authentic Mexican food, at least until my butt builds up a tolerance.

Puerto Ricans, *por lo* general, don't know a thing about Mexican food. We don't cook with *chiles*. And, authentic or not, our systems can be overwhelmed by it pretty easily. To say the least, it's got more of a kick than Puerto Rican food.

We took my grandmother to a Mexican restaurant for her 89th birthday. She lived, but *esa noche la pasó* in the emergency room. And she had ordered the "mild" *enchiladas*. But that's how you really rate Mexican food. *Si terminas en el hospital*, that's fantastic Mexican food. If it kills you, even better. Multiple casualties, *olvídate*, that's the best that you can get.

The way Mexicans make beans is also different from the way we Puerto Ricans make our beans. First of all, we call them *habichuelas* and they call them *frijoles*. And we would never eat them refried, which we regard as *el colmo* of culinary blasphemy. Not that we have anything against frying.

It's just that the texture is so mushy that we don't even recognize them as beans *cuando se preparan así*. The first time I ordered rice and beans at a Mexican restaurant, I remember how shocked I was when they brought me my plate. I wanted *habichuelas*, not a bean smoothie poured over in the corner like a stool sample from a rabbit with the runs.

My girlfriend, *quien es mexicana*, explained that Mexicans prepare refried beans with lard, and that's why they're like that. Whatever. To a Puerto Rican, it just tastes like, "What went wrong?"

Sometimes a *Pupusa* Is Just a *Pupusa*

Now the Salvadorean *pupusa* is a Latino food name that really fooled me the first time I heard it. I was on a first date with a woman in San Francisco, and she says to me, "*¿Quieres una pupusa?*" And I thought, "Wow, this girl must really be digging me. Normally, I have to work a lot harder to get that kind of offer. Must be the new cologne."

My father cracked up so hard when I told him that. And afterward he would always ask me, "*Oye*, Billy, how's the *pupusa* in San Francisco?"

Oh, and before *que se me olvide*, if you're *watcheando* your calories, *te tengo unas muy buenas noticias*. At least you don't have to totally give up on pork chops. I will soon be marketing my *chuletas* made out of tofu. I'm calling them *tofuletas!* They'll be available at *la* Trader Joes.

TOP TEN SPANGLISH ICE CREAM FLAVORS

1. *COCOTAZO* COCONUT CRUNCH

2. *PAPI CHULO* PAPAYA

3. *VIRGEN DE GUACAMOLE* AVOCADO

4. DOUBLE CHUNKY *CHICHARRÓN*

5. *PURO POCHO* CHOCOLATE CHIP

6. CELIA CRUZ'S "*¡AZÚCAR!*" ATTACK *TAMARINDO*

7. *DULCE DE PORQUE* BECAUSE

8. *RECONQUISTA* ROCKY ROAD

9. *COJONES* AND CREAM MACHISMO SUPREME

10. CHUPACABRABERRY

BONUS: WALTER MERCADO TUTTI FRUTTI

7

LOVE IN THE TIME OF
PORQUE BECAUSE

¿Qué más quieres? **I'm single, bilingual,** *y estoy listo* **to mingle.**
—Spanglish pickup line

When it comes to *cosas románticas*, we the people of *la vida loca* get deep into Spanglish. In the throes of *flechazo* fever, *enredados como* pretzels, whispering sweet *nadas* to our *media naranjas*, only Spanglish lets us properly verbalize the bilingual *latidos* of our *corazones*.

Lust *a primera vista*, harmless *coqueteo*, unrequited *piropeo*, and every other kind of love in the time of *porque* because all find inspired expression in the *habla*.

Me urge subrayar que Spanglish not only lends itself *al romance* but sparks it. *Porque, como bien sabido es, lo prohibido provoca.* The very act of speaking it is taboo, as if English and Spanish were cousins forbidden to be cavorting together. And yet, as the saying goes, *el primo a la prima se le arrima.*

This subconscious sense of illicitness kicks any *flirteo* up a notch, compelling legions *de los nuestros* to kiss, and eventually tell, in Spanglish.

Es más, the best Spanglish involving *temas de amor se escucha cuando* we get debriefed by friends and family about our latest *aventuras* and *fracasos.* Stories *de cómo te dejaron* brokenhearted, *de* how you met, *de cómo te fue* last night, *de que si* it's the real thing *o sólo un* fling, spew forth in *idioma*-switching gabfests.

Enjoy the following soundbites from *la esfera de los enamorados.*

ESTABLISHING BOUNDARIES

"*Hazme un favor* and don't be such a *pulpo.* Keep your hands to yourself."

ÚLTIMO ULTIMATUM

"*Tenemos que casarnos* this year. *Porque si* no, then it's 'OK, good-bye.'"

¡QUE VIVA MAE WEST*!*

"Is that a *plátano* in your pocket, or are you just *muy* happy to see me?"

CHOOSE YOUR *PALABRAS* CAREFULLY

"*Entonces,* I said to her, *le dije,* 'Look, I want kids *pero no contigo.*' That's when she broke everything in my apartment. *Y después me puse a pensar,* "Did I say something wrong?'"

PUES NADA, THAT'S THE STORY

"*Bueno, estábamos como los* Three Stooges, *jugando* all the time, *y esto y lo otro,* and we became real good friends *y empezamos a salir. Y él se enamoró, pero bien enamorado,* and me too. *Lo único que* he's got problems with alcohol. *Y yo me dije, pues,* nobody's perfect. *Entonces el tipo me salió con que* we couldn't have sex for six months! *Me tenía sufriendo* and I started to worry *que* maybe *no podía cumplir en la cama y se había vuelto* impotent from all the drinking. *Pero ¡qué va!* Last Saturday *nos entregamos en la playa, a lo* 'Blue Lagoon,' *bajo una luna llena* and he's fine. He is fine! *Muchacho, estamos disfrutando un montón.* The wait was worth it. *Te digo que* I felt like a virgin, *te lo juro,* really."

UNA SENIOR SEXY

"See her out there on the balcony, with the grey hair? *Está madura, pero todavía aguanta sus pingazos.*"

AND, HE CROSSES HIS LEGS

"*Perdona, chico, no te quise ofender.* It's just that since you never made a pass at me, *pensé que eras del otro* way. Not that there's anything wrong with that."

NEVER LET THEM SEE YOU SWEAT

"**She's a little high maintenance.** *'De ésas que cuando se agitan sudan* **Channel Number Three."***

UNDERSTATEMENT

"**She took off her shirt,** *y me dice,* **'Well, what do you think?'** *Tenía unos senos tan preciosos que me quedé en* **shock!** *Y al fin le contesté,* **'Not bad.'"**

TELL IT TO THE JUDGE

"**You taped her** *sin su consentimiento en actos sexuales, deplorables y repugnantes. Por lo tanto,* **I find you guilty.** *No sólo de ser un criminal, sino también un* **real jerk.** *¡Caso cerrado!"*

FAIR WARNING

"*Pobre de ti, si estás* **cheating on me,** *porque mi papi* **will come after you with his** *escopeta.*"

PLEASE DON'T TEASE *LOS LOBOS*

"*No puedes mirarme así con esos ojos tan deseosos y negarme un beso.* **That's false advertising.**"

---

*This "Channel Number Three" line is actually from one of my favorite Ruben Blades songs ever, *"Plástico,"* a very funny and scathing indictment of superficiality. It's a great example too of how, in Spanglish usage, brand names mostly get left as is. Plus, not only does it work lyrically, but by keeping the brand name in English, Blades emphasizes the empty shishiness, or *mejor dicho, the comemierda*-ness, he wants to condemn in a more comedic way.

HIJO DE GATO

"He's a *corazón* breaker. *Otro picaflor como su papá.* "

EASY COME, EASY GO

"*Entonces* we hit it off, *tú sabes. Pero* he's back in rehab. *Te lo digo que* I've had some winners."

¡QUÉ EXAGERADO!

"No more Internet dating. *En su post de* Cragslist, *el muy sinvergüenza dijo que tenía un* 'swimmer's body.' *¡Mentira!* Well, *digo,* unless he meant as in '*manatí.*' "

SWEET MEMORIES

"Oh it's a love story. She knew I was in this crew of gangsters, right, and she found out that I was the main *chingón* and couldn't resist my *chingonerías.* So I remember one year, *le di una llamadita* to come over and watch 'It's a Wonderful Life,' 'cause, you wouldn't think so, *pero* it's my favorite movie, right, especially in black and white and shit, and I didn't want to see it alone. Actually, *fue un* Christmas booty call. And we've been *chingando* ever since."

BUT WE ONLY HOOKED UP ONCE

"Congratulations. *Te echaste un gol en la primera jugada.* I've always been like that, though. *Caigo en cinta sólo de ver unos calzoncillos.* "

TEMPTING, BUT *NO, GRACIAS*

"Quería llevarme skinny dipping *¡Imagínate!* On the first date. *Y yo estaba como que,* 'Should I do it?' *Pero, no mija no, lo siento, pero yo no soy tan* open minded."

KEEPING SCORE

"I wouldn't call it true love. More like, *amor deportivo.* One thing led to another *y nos fuimos pa'* extra innings."

¿WHY TAN TRISTE?

"Hey Gladys. *¿Qué te pasa?* You sound sad. *¿Y qué pasó con* Mr. Midlife Crisis? *'Dito.* But why were you crying? Get out of here. *¡Pues, divórciate ya! Y dale gracias a Dios que* you never signed that friggin' prenup."

REDEEMING QUALITIES

"Feo de vicio, pero tenemos chemistry."

"I WILL SURVIVE"

Lyrics by Frederick J. Perron and Dino Fekaris; recorded by Gloria Gaynor

Spanglish translation *por* Bill Santiago

First I was afraid

Estuve petrified

Kept thinking *no podría vivir*

sin tenerte by my side

Pero pasé so many nights

thinking *que eras un cabrón*

Me puse strong

Aprendí cómo to carry on

Y pues, you're back

desde el outer space

Entré y te encontré

con ese sad look upon *tu* face

Debería haber changed *mi* stupid lock

Y las keys *hacerte devolver*

If I had known for just one second

you'd be back *para joder*

Pues vete go. *Ahí está la* door

just turn around now

Aquí no estás welcome anymore

¿Tú no fuiste quien quería hurt me *con* goodbye?

¿Pensaste que I'd crumble, *ah?*

¿Que me iba a lay down and die?

¡Jamás! Not I

Voy a survive

As long *que yo sepa* how to love

Sé que voy a stay alive

Tengo all my life to live

Todo mi corazón to give

Y voy a survive

Voy a survive

Dios mío qué lucha era

not to fall apart

¿Cómo sanar los pedacitos

de mi broken heart?

And I spent oh so many nights

pobrecita, by myself.

I used to cry

Y al fin me dije, "Wait a second, *estás* high?"

Y tú me ves

Soy alguien new

I'm not *la misma pendejita*

still in love with you

¡Qué sinvergüenza! dropping in

esperando que yo estuviera free

Well, I'm saving *mis caricias*

para mi nuevo honey . . .

Frequently Asked *Preguntas*

1. P: Is Spanglish the new Yiddish?

A: Yes, in fact, there's a Latino newspaper called *"Hoy,"* which used to be called "Oy." It's been a pretty smooth transition, actually. Occasionally, I still find myself translating between the two languages. The other night I said to my girlfriend, "You're such a pain in the *tuchas!*" And she said, "What's *tuchas?*" And I explained, "It's Yiddish for *fundillo.*" So I would agree. Spanglish is the new Yiddish. *Cojones* is the new chutzpah. And Latinos are the new chosen *gente.*

2. P: Wasn't there a movie called "Spanglish"?

A: Yes, but there wasn't any actual Spanglish in it. *¡Imagínate!* It was like going to see a movie called "Star Wars," *lo único que* there's no stars and no wars, just two *borrachos discutiendo* whether or not Pluto is a planet. Oh, and the Latina maid character, *pues ella*, she really broke new ground, *tú sabes.* I'm glad they didn't rehash any stereotypes.

3. P: Is there a secret Spanglish agenda?

A: Well, after "Dora the Explorer," I don't think it's so secret anymore. *Pero*, yes. We demand liberation and *amnistía total* for the rebel alliance leaders who hijacked Air Force One and forced *El Pendejo Jr.* to sing the "Star-Spanglish Banner." We want driver's tests to be offered in Spanglish. We want the ñ to be mandatory on computer keyboards. And we want Ben and Jerry's to offer Spanglish ice cream flavors. That's *nuestra agenda.*

4. P: Can deaf people sign in Spanglish?

A: Yes, and you can tell when they are signing the Spanish words, too, because the gestures suddenly get all crazy and emotional, *casi como si fuera un* epileptic fit.

5. P: Why is Spanglish so funny?

A: *Porque* because.

6. P: So what language do you actually think in?

A: Well, it really depends on the last language you were operating in. There's a little bit of a lag. Like I was reading this ad for the Army but it was in Spanish. So instead of "I Am Army," it said "*Soy* Army." Then I walked into a Starbucks and there was a sign that said: "Soy Milk." So, you know, in my head I understood it as "I Am Milk," because my brain hadn't switched over yet into English. I was still in the military context. "Reporting for duty, Sir. Ready to unleash hell on those lactose intolerant sons of bitches."

The Joy of *Chisme*

Chisme* is a highly concentrated form of gossip enjoyed by Latinos *que no pueden* mind *su* own business. Unlike gossip, *chisme* is never idle.

It's like the double-espresso of gossip that gets you buzzed on the buzz of other people's private lives and without which *la vida sería aburridísima*.

My girlfriend, who just hung up the phone shouting, "Jackpot!" after scoring some *chisme gordo*, admits it's one of her biggest thrills. "I don't know, it's like insider trading," she says. "You've got this secret, highly valuable information and just anticipating, you know, the effect that it's going to have when

* *Chisme* is pronounced "cheese-may."

you tell it to somebody else . . . it's such a rush!"

To get the full benefits of full-frontal Spanglish *chisme*, it must be conducted sparing no embarrassing detail about the *pocas vergüenzas* of family, friends, neighbors, colleagues, and strangers. Indulge shamelessly, remembering it's not *chisme* unless you mention shame, specifically *la falta de vergüenza*, at least *mil veces*.

Pepper your *chisme* with phrases like: "¡What a *sinvergüenza!*" "¡No tiene nada de vergüenza*, at all!" "Why would anybody put up *con esas pocas vergüenzas?*" "¡Oye, es verdad que ya la gente no tiene shame!"*

Chisme Central

All the best *chisme* is preceded by a variation of the following warning: "But don't tell anybody, *porque si no, no te digo más nada* ever again." This isn't meant to actually stop you from blabbing the highly sensitive information you're being entrusted with. *Sólo te deja saber que* something *escandaloso* and worth repeating *viene por ahí*. In fact, you are then expected to immediately tell everyone you know, *quizás* as a mass e-mail blast to save time. Just put "*chisme*" in the subject line and it's bound to go viral.

A little shock value goes a long way, but any mildly juicy tidbit is legitimate grist for the *chisme* mill.

Always strive to deliver your *chisme* with an animated tone, using plenty of hand gestures, facial expressions (eye rolling, very good), *pero siempre en manera* hush-hush. And remember: There's no such thing as "*demasiada información.*"

---

*The "*sh*" in shame, when used for *chisme* purposes, is pronounced like the "*ch*" in *chisme*.

For inspiration about content, *estudien los ejemplos siguientes*:

BLANCA TO NANCY ABOUT STEVE

"*Válgame Dios,* I saw him in a pool. In a bathing suit. *Tenía una espalda de oso.* And he's the one who's always hitting on me at work. *Pero, lo siento,* that's a deal breaker. *Yo no me puedo acostar con nadie así de* hairy."

MARÍA TO RAQUEL ABOUT BLANCA

"Oh, they're not real. *¡Qué va!* She told me herself. *Se hizo las tetas,* and she got one of those *panza*-tucks too. *¿Y ese culazo? Olvídate,* not hers either. Not only that—*y esto no se lo vayas a repetir a nadie*—she paid for it all *con un* home-improvement loan. *Dice que* if she looks better, *pues entonces que la casa está* improved."

RAUL TO JACKIE ABOUT RICARDO

"*Es un adicto total al* gambling *pero está en* denial. *Tuvo que* file for bankruptcy *después de que* he lost *como* twenty thousand dollars *jugando al* poker. *¡Imagínate tú, cargado a su* credit card! *Pero entonces* he got a lot of frequent-flyer miles for it. So you know what he does? *El muy sinvergüenza ése* uses the miles *para volver a* Las Vegas!"

TITI ROSA TO NELSON, CARMEN, AND LUPITA ABOUT JAVIER AND VICKY

"Cuando I saw those pictures, *me dije,* 'wait a minute.' *Se ve más redondita* and she has no waist. And there's Javi *tocándole la barriga.* I'm telling you, *la muchacha se dejo preñar de* Javi *para atraparlo.* There's a baby on the way."

SAM TO TANIA ABOUT PILAR

"Te digo que lately, *esa* Pilar is getting on my nerves. *Ayer* we were supposed to meet for drinks *con una* client at Frontera Grill, *y se le olvidó por completo,* never showed up. Seriously, *ella es una verdadera* flakeasaurus."

RUBY TO DENISE ABOUT JESSY

"And then what's with that new guy she's with? *¡Un hombre casado* who just got out of jail! She tells me, *'A veces uno tiene que tomar riesgos, ¿no?'* And I'm thinking, 'That's not a *riesgo,* that's just stupid.' *Pero* she doesn't care. *No tiene orgullo, y la pobrecita está* messing up *su* life. *Pero* anyway, *a mi no me gusta estar hablando mal de nadie."*

Chisme stimulates production of endorphins, relieves stress, and boosts the immune system. I bet *que no lo sabían!* It also promotes social bonding, provides endless hours of entertainment, and is a great way to keep up your Spanglish chops.

And don't feel any guilt or *vergüenza* when partaking in *chisme* about others, because at this very moment, *puedes estar muy seguro,* somebody is *chis-*

meando big time about you.

The Unbearable Lightness of "*Cójelo** *con* Take It Easy"

I gotta be honest with you, "*Cójelo con* take it easy," makes me very uneasy. It defies comprehension, which may be what makes it *un dicho tan clásico del* Spanglish. What the hell does it mean, exactly? *Generaciones futuras* will still be asking.

Cuando este disparate popular se traduce back into English, it literally means, "Take it with take it easy." *Lo cual* makes no sense whatsoever. You can turn it over any way you want, *pero no tiene sentido.*

But Spanglish speakers, *sin embargo,* go right ahead and say this phrase as if it makes total sense, *a veces* as a form of "good-bye," *pero* mostly *para significar* "chill out" or "relax" or "lighten up" or "don't take it too seriously."

I personally can't take anyone who says it seriously because it sounds so retarded.

Ah, *pero* that's the beauty of it.

The phrase has a strange suggestive power to chill you out *precisamente* because it makes no literal sense whatsoever. *De hecho,* it has been proven that you can relieve stress simply by saying, "*Cójelo con* take it easy" over and over as a mantra. This flushes the mind out thoroughly with unintelligible nonsense *para que puedas olvidar* your worries.

Try it, and thank me *después.*

---

*Officially, "*cojer*" is spelled "*coger*" with a "g." But when you're *cojiéndolo con* take it easy, spelling's the first thing to slip through the cracks. *Por lo tanto,* out of respect for popular usage and abusage, I am deliberately and of my own volition sticking with "j" for *nuestros* purposes *aquí.*

Mutant Rise of a *Disparate*

But the bigger question still remains: How did something as ridiculous sounding as "*Cójelo con* take it easy" ever get coined in the first place? *¿De dónde* does it come from? Why has it been adopted as one of the most popular Spanglish sayings ever?

The short answer is *porque* because. But since I'm writing a book here, *entraremos en un poquito más de detalle sobre la cuestión.* Besides, aren't you dying to know?

Let's back up a little bit and start with what we do know.

The American colloquialism "take it easy" begat the Spanish translation "*cójelo suave,*" which begat the Spanglish translation "*cójelo* easy," which . . . and here it's anybody's guess what happened next. I mean it's a real mystery. But if there is one possible linguistic missing link, I think we can find it in the Spanish colloquialism "*Cójelo con calma.*" Which translates literally into "take it with calm" but is generally understood to mean "Don't forget to take your Prozac," and it is the official Spanish counterpart to "take it easy."

Following me so far?

At some point in Spanglish history, the two colloquialisms must have been crossed!

Somebody meant to say "*cójelo* easy" but realized too late that he was already three-quarters of the way into saying "*cójelo con calma.*" Of course, he didn't take it *con calma* at all but freaked at "*cójelo con,*" and he blurted out the now infamous midsentence do-over "take it easy" to finish his thought by reverting to the original untranslated English phrase he wanted to Spanglishize in the first place.*

His friends probably fell over *meándose de la risa* and never let him forget it, not realizing he was a bilingual pioneer.

Aside from not making sense, the phrase *nos causa risa por muchas otras razones.* Not the least of which is because some Spanish-speaking peoples regard the verb *coger* as an obscenity, meaning to fornicate.

While I personally wouldn't think twice about saying "*Voy a coger un taxi,*" in some Latin American countries that might be interpreted as quite a sexual fetish, and cabbies would probably want to charge extra.

A safer substitute for *coger* might have been *tomar,* resulting in "*tómalo easy.*" But Spanglish has never been about being safe, so this option got relatively little traction.

"Take it *suave,*" although legitimate, never caught on among Latinos either, because it sounds, well, *demasiado gringo,* according to most surveys. (I only asked one person, *pero* we both agreed *que* I was right.)

Ultimately, "*Cójelo con* take it easy" stuck not only because it was hilarious and infectiously absurd, but because it could have come only from a Spanglish culture. And so we claim it *orgullosamente.* It's exclusively and indigenously ours, *este bendito disparate,* and the millions of people who use it every day are all in on the joke.

---

*This theory is based on exhaustive research by the *Cójelo Con* Take It Easy Think Tank at the Santiago Spanglish Institute for World Peace and is the best damn explanation I've heard so far. Also, note that variations such as "*Cójelo con mucho* take it easy" (a little more insistent) and "*Cójelo suave con* take it easy" (a little more redundant)—although not as common—have also been documented.

TOP TEN WAYS TO USE "*CÓJELO CON* TAKE IT EASY" IN A SENTENCE

1. TAKE A DEEP BREATH, AND *CÓJELO CON* TAKE IT EASY *O VAS A TENER UN* HEART ATTACK.

2. *¡AY, NO SEAS TAN* SENSITIVE! *CÓJELO CON* TAKE IT EASY, *PORQUE TÚ SABES QUE* I WAS ONLY JOKING.

3. NO WORRIES. *CÓJELO CON* TAKE IT EASY, BROSKI.

4. STAY TUNED AND *CÓJELO CON* TAKE IT EASY WHILE WE PAUSE FOR A WORD FROM OUR SPONSORS.

5. THIS IS THE POLICE! COME OUT WITH YOUR HANDS UP AND *CÓJELO CON* TAKE IT EASY!

6. FEELING JITTERY FROM TOO MUCH CAFFEINE? TRY "*CÓJELO CON* TAKE IT EASY" DECAF!

7. AND A BIG "*CÓJELO CON* TAKE IT EASY" TO YOU TOO.

8. THANK YOU FOR ELECTING ME PRESIDENT. GOD BLESS AMERICA, AND *CÓJELO CON* TAKE IT EASY.

9. *¿CÓMO QUE* TIRED? ALL YOU DO IS SIT AROUND AND *CÓJELO CON* TAKE IT EASY ALL DAY.

10. AND ON THE SEVENTH DAY, GOD DECIDED TO *CÓJELO CON* TAKE IT EASY.

8

SPANGLISH ON THE JOB,

ON THE *BÉISBOL* FIELD, AND ON THE RUNWAY

Fue un mistay.

—Sammy Sosa, after getting caught *corkeando* his bat

On the Job Spanglish

Spanglish works great at work. Cubicles everywhere are crackling with the *habla,* as embedded Latinos, *aumentando exponencialmente su presencia* in the white-collar ranks, make the offices of corporate America particularly Spanglish-rich *ambientes.*

By the way, I happen to be writing this on a Wednesday. So *¡Feliz* hump day!

Spanglish improves morale, facilitates cohesion, sparks innovation, *incrementa* customer loyalty. Or*, por lo menos,* provides a perfect way for bilingual drones *de la oficina* to vent, whine, rant, and, of course, *chismear* about workplace goings-on. So either way, *es una solución de* win-win.

I had a great time putting together *los siguientes ejemplos* and recommend you read them *en voz alta*, at work, *para disfrutar a lo máximo*. Now then, *veamos cómo los* Spanglishistas *del* 9-to-5, employees, managers, and *los* head honchos *más altos* all over the country, *se aprovechan del* business *idioma* of *mañana*, today.*

NETWORKING

"That's how you get ahead. *Mucho schmoozeo.*"

CORPORATE STRATEGY

"*Te digo que* the merger *con* Cuchifrito Corp. *me pareció un* no-brainer, *porque* we've got to stay competitive. *Camarón que se duerme se lo lleva la corriente.* But the top brass didn't go for it. *¡Otro* great idea *que me fusilan!*"

POST-VACATION BLUES

"I got back two days ago. *Y todavía estoy hasta las narices en* backed up e-mails."

COWORKER APPRECIATION

"Speaking of *culo*, look who's bending over at the water cooler."

---

*I always thought that the term "head honcho" derived from Spanish origins. But I was *el wrong-o*. The word *honcho* traces back to the Japanese term for "squadron leader" and was adopted by American servicemen during *La Segunda Guerra Mundial*. When speaking Spanglish, *honcho* still sounds Spanish enough for me. But alternately you can use *"jefazo," "el mero mero,"* or *"el* big *queso."*

NEW COMPANY POLICY

"Bueno, and right in the middle of it *es que llega mi boss y estábamos como* as if we were working hard, *tú sabes,* and not playing fantasy baseball. *Menos mal que* we didn't get busted *porque* we're not allowed to goof off anymore. It's a zero tolerance anti-*goofeo* crackdown."

PRIORITIES

"FYI, I need the SOP ASAP. And pronto. Comprende?"

APPROPRIATE WARDROBE

"Mija, a veces the difference between a good raise and a great raise is a little *pechonalidad.* So don't worry about *demasiado* cleavage."

SAYING *BASTA YA*

"Voy a quitear el trabajo and retire. *Estoy* burned out."

LET'S SHOW THEM WHO'S *NÚMERO UNO*

"Johnson, the client wants the whole *enchilada* on this project. Crank it out by *mañana,* or he goes *loco* and we're both in deep *caca.* But pull it off, and I'll make you *el jefe* of your department, making *mucho dinero,* I might add."

JOB ENVY

"No te quejes. I wish I had your job. *Sería un mamey."*

AN OFFER YOU CAN REFUSE

"Hoy mismo me llamó un headhunter to ask for my resume *y le dije que no me interesa ser ningún* cubicle monkey. Been there, done that. *Es un poco difícil vivir* from job to job. *Pero con el* freelancing at least *puedo trabajar* from home *y hasta en mi* underwear *si me da la gana."*

SIZING UP *LA* NEW *JEFA*

"She's 29, *apenas, la cabrona.* Younger than me *y además es una* ball buster. Oh my God, walking around *como si fuera* Donald Trump, *'¡Estás* fired! *¡Estás* fired! *¡Estás* fired!' *Olvídate, y cómo le encantan los* meetings. Meetings and meetings. *Estoy mareada de tantos* meetings, for real *te lo juro.* Every day *me pregunto,* 'Should I go to work? *O debo de* call in sick?' Hopefully, I get fired next, *porque para mí sería un* good news."

IRONY OF IT ALL

"Fíjate que en el trabajo no le dan ningunos benefits, *pero el* boss *de ella la tiene como una* friend *con* benefits."

DIVERSITY

"Están constantemente on my case about getting to work on

time, *a pesar de que* they recruited me *porque querían* a 'native Spanish speaker' in that position. *Pues,* if they want diversity, *entonces tienen que* deal *con el* cultural bagagge. Right? *Voy a tener que demandarlos por* punctual harassment.''

Spanglish for a Whole Different *Béisbol* Game

¿Qué tal baseball fans*?* If Spanglish thrives in any sport, it's got to be in *el béisbol.* When I listen to a game on the radio, I can't tell anymore if I've tuned in an English or Spanish broadcast, *porque* because the announcers *siempre están* mixing *los* languages *tan* furiously.

On a Spanish *emisora* I'll hear: "*La segunda* double play. *Hay dos* outs, *dos eh*-strikes, *una bola . . .*"

Then, I'll switch over to an English station:" . . . and Alex Rodríguez says *adiós* to *la pelotah!*"

America's official *pasatiempo nacional* happens to provide optimal conditions for Spanglish. It's a hyper-bilingual environment featuring a sport with original terminology in English and a tsunami of Latino *peloteros*, where announcers and *comentaristas* have to talk as fast as possible *para poder* keep up *con lo que está* going on.

Check out these choice snippets from two different games chosen at random. The first I heard on a Spanish radio show, the second on an English-language station.

BASEBALL *EN ESPAÑOL*

"*Envío en camino . . . el* swing *y un batazo hacia* right field! *Se va, se va, se va, se vaaaaaa . . . y se fue!* ¡*Jonrón!* con **bases loaded** *de* **Hideki Mastui!** ¡*Pegándose un* **grand slam!** *Y la tortilla se ha volteado aquí en* **El Bronx,** *así que nos vamos para* **extra innings!** ¡*Hideki Matsui!* ¡*Este* **Bud** *es para* **you!**"

BÉISBOL IN ENGLISH

"**Strike three!** ¿*Qué pasa* with *El Papí?* He's coming up with a whole lotta *nada!*"

I don't even care who's winning or losing games anymore, I'm so busy keeping *eh*-score of how much Spanglish is being tossed around *el diamante.* Here are some of my favorite sound bites, weighted individually for Spanglish Slugging Average (*béisbol's* newest official statistic) based on effectiveness, creativity, degree of difficulty, and originality.

BASES LOADED IN SPANGLISH

"Jeter *en* short *captura el* pop fly, *fácil para este tremendo fieldeador . . . * " (.450)

"*Un* wild pitch! *El* bullpen *de* Pittsburgh *está fallando . . . * " (.275)

"Join us for post-game *mojitos* and martinis." (.220)

"*El* umpire *concede un* time out." (.310)

"Robinson *levanta un flycito cómodo al* infield, Abreu *lo catcha y dispara al* homeplate *para el* double play *que termina el* inning." (.510)

"Where's the defense? Are they taking a *siesta* out there?" (.190)

"*¡Otro cudrangular del jonrronero* Barry Bonds *cae con un* splash *en el Eh*-Steroid Cove*!*" (.490)

"And the White Sox sweep the World Series! *¡Que viva* Chicago! *¡Que viva el* Southside!"(.375)

"*El Duque logra un casi* perfect game *con una verdadera joya de pitcheo . . .* " (.410)

"And the capacity crowd at Cuchifrito Corp. Stadium is going completely *loco!*" (.390)

I've never heard any announcer choke during a bilingual play by play, either. *Algunos* seriously *merecen* to be inducted into the Spanglish *Salón de Fama* for the way they so artfully handle any and all combinations as *territorio* fair. *¡Nunca levantan un* foul!

Fashionably Spanglish

A veces Spanglish is only skin deep, all about *el nuevo* look, *el* look *más* sexy, *el último* look, *el* look *más* "in."

On any given magazine rack, *se encuentran* dozens of *Cosmo*-cloned *revistas*, offering *unos* tips *de belleza, secretos de los mejores* personal trainers, and maybe a headline on the cover, asking, *"¿Eres Una* Fashion Victim*?"*

Makes sense, *¿verdad?* How could a language as fashionable as Spanglish not come into play *cuando se está hablando de* fashion? *Por lo tanto,* an entire branch of the *habla* is dedicated to *cómo ser más* hot.

Or in the case of my Titi Norma, *cómo de* hot she used to be. *En su época,* during her pinup, head-turning glory days of the '60s, *tenía* the body of a Latina goddess that raised temperatures even in Hell's Kitchen, *y una cara* that launched a thousand *barrio*-mobiles.

She loves to show off the old pictures of herself taken back then, impossibly young and posing so coquettishly for the lens. And as we stare she comments with wonderfully self-deprecating humor.

> **"Back in the day, your *titi* was beautiful. *Ahora parezco que me pasó un* truck *por encima*. What happen, right?"**

But a little Spanglish can do wonders for your image. *Uno se puede hacer un* makeover. *O sólo darse los toquecitos de* maintenance *de vez en cuando. Puedes* try *un* cream *de* anti-aging *para borrar las arrugas.* Or you can go under the knife, *para conseguir la pechonalidad* you always wanted.

And as far as fitness goes, if all else fails, try denial: "*Yo no estoy gorda. Es que tengo algunos* fat deposits *en mis caderas.*"

At least *nuestra cultura* appreciates *mujeres buenotas de* full-figure. Real women have curves *y no tienen que estar* counting calories. Still, take it easy *con el* junk food *y asegúrate de vestir* appropriately for your figure. *Nada se ve* worse, *que una mujer media* chubby *en unos* jeans *muy* low cut, *resultando en el odioso* muffin top.

Men are just as *vanidosos* these days. And they're generating just as much Spanglish about staying in shape, *haciendo sus* pushups *para ponerse bien toneados y evitar los* man boobs.

Now, Spanglish exercise is certainly making great strides. Yes, you too can have the derriere *de tus* dreams with *Pompilates!* This revolutionary new system, harnessing *el poder* of pilates *para tus pompis*, is even more popular than those

"*Nalgas* of Steel" videos. Above all, *lo importante es ser* realistic. Don't compare yourself to *esas* cover girls *que ni siquiera se ven así* in person. Keep in mind *que sus* picture-perfect *imágenes* are courtesy of *el photoshopeo.*

We all know *que* true *belleza* starts on the inside. But since that's rarely enough, *tienes que* pamper the outside *lo más posible. No dejes de hacerte el* manicure, *el* pedicure, *un* facial, *y darte un* nice massage. And *entonces*, every once in a while, *sométete a un buen* waxing, Brazilian, *si te atreves. Dolerá algo brutal,* from what I hear.

In my personal experience, fashion talk is inseparable from girlfriend talk when it comes to the *habla* so you can guess the source of the following examples.

- "There is a super sexy dress on sale. *Si me lo vieras puesto,* you couldn't resist me."

- "*Estos* jeans *me quedan* sprayed on."

- "*El color de* shocking pink *está muy de moda,* so I never wear it."

- "Mmmm, I don't know, *me siento disfrazada. Este* outfit *no es mi* look."

- "*Mira,* we're both wearing blue. *Sin querer queriendo,* we match!"

- "*Dame cinco minutitos* and I'll be ready to go. I just have to *shinear mis* shoes."

- "Don't you wish *que tu* girlfriend *fuera* hot like me . . . oh, but she is, *qué suerte tienes . . .* "

TOP TEN BEST THINGS ABOUT SPANGLISH

1. NOT TAUGHT IN SCHOOLS, SO YOU CAN NEVER FLUNK SPANGLISH.

2. *LO PUEDES HACER* BY ACCIDENT.

3. COMES IN HANDY WHEN TRAVELING IN SPANGLISH-SPEAKING COUNTRIES.

4. BOOSTS YOUR *BARRIO* STREET CRED.

5. YOU DON'T HAVE TO SPEAK GOOD ENGLISH OR GOOD SPANISH TO BE COMPLETELY FLUENT IN SPANGLISH.

6. IT'S TITILLATING. NOT AS TITILLATING AS ACTUAL TITS, BUT CLOSE.

7. GIVES YOU COMPETITIVE EDGE IN SPANGLISH SCRABBLE.

8. AS A FULL-FLEDGED SPANGLISH SPEAKER, YOU'RE GOING TO SOUND *MÁS* COOL. WAY *MÁS!*

9. TWICE THE ANTIOXIDANT POWER OF POMEGRANATE JUICE.

10. IT'S EASIER THAN CHINGLISH!

9

SPANGLISH
¡O MUERTE!

¿Is it me, or does it smell like *azufre* in here?

—Hugo Chávez on the White House tour

Some people are very anti-Spanglish. In fact, *les da asco*. It makes them sick to their *estómagos* and nearly barf their *lonche*.

English and Spanish extremists everywhere have got their *chonies* (as my Chicano friends *suelen decir*) all in a bunch about it. Spanish-purist ayatollahs *hasta se han unido con los* English-only *jihadistas* in issuing a big fat *fatwahtazo* declaring death *a todos los* Spanglish infidels.

Which, at least to me, begs an obvious question.

¿Por qué the hate, dudes? I mean really. *No es pa' tanto*.

Yet these fundamentalists react *como si el* Spanglish *fuera* not only an insult to their mother tongues *pero sino también* to their actual mothers. *Les parece tan y tan* wrong, a deviant behavior *tan repugnante*, a dangerous and unforgivable *barbaridad* so cancerous *que* they will stop at *nada* to make it stop.

Backlash of the Fundamentalists

As Spanglish grows, *así mismo crece el* backlash against it. But we the persecuted *tenemos que ser firme.* Such *intolerancia* must only gird us with strength unto *la batalla.* If enemies of the *habla* want to burn this book in mass protest, for instance, *digo yo,* "bring it on." *Bueno, porque la verdad del caso es que* you can't buy that kind of publicity. *Es más, yo mismo prendo el fósforo.*

But again, *para que estemos claro,* the opposition has two faces. On the Spanish side, *nuestro* beloved Spanglish *tiene cierta fama,* not as a lingua franca, but rather a lingua *fracasada.*

Spanglish drives defenders of "pure" Spanish nuts, *amenazando la sensibilidad de los más dogmáticos* because it disgusts them as a horribly deformed variation of *español,* totally *podrido de americanismos, anglicismos,* and *palabras sajonas.* They particularly resent English, *como el idioma que manda,* the bully of all languages, *mezclándose tan descaradamente* with their own precious *idioma* and culture.

Más aún, they love to ridicule Spanglish *como una forma inferior de comunicación,* and as virtual *analfabetismo.* Which strikes me as cluelessly cocky. It's kind of like a snobby stork *burlándose de como vuelan los* hummingbirds. "You call that flying?" *le dice la cigüeña al colibrí.* "Listen, it doesn't qualify as real flying unless you can deliver a baby, OK? Speaking of which, I gotta go. Miss García is expecting twins for her *quinceañera.*"

Spanglish Envy

In the United States, *cuna del* Spanglish, the English-only supremacists hate any Spanish being spoken at all. If they had it their way, uttering so much as a "*Dios mío*," in public would be enough to get you deported.

If you come to live *en este país*, giving up your Spanish is the price you pay, according to *estos yanquis ultraconservadores* and minute-men *colaboracionistas*. Don't be trying to sneak in your contraband *español* as Spanglish, either. *Por lo tanto*, Spanish fraternizing with English *de cualquier manera* whatsoever, especially after 9/11, *no se debe permitir.*

Boy, I'll tell you what I think all this hate and blanket dismissal is really about. Clearly, enemies of the *habla* suffer from severe Spanglish-envy. *Así es.* These *celosos babosos* are just jealous of our *doble pertenencia lingüística* and wish they could go back and forth *como nosotros.*

In any case, *los enemigos del* Spanglish cannot win. *La suya es una lucha perdida de antemano.* You might be able to stop global warming, but Spanglish just isn't going away *así de fácil*. If you think otherwise, I suggest you curb your *entusiasmo.*

Grammar nazis and lexical fascists take note. Languages change, they evolve. *¿Cuál es el* big issue? *Sin esta dinámica de transformación, adaptación, experimentación y cambio, no existiría ni* English, *ni* Spanish. We don't have to surrender or apologize to the high priests of any language, especially those who like to chalk up Spanglish to *pereza mental.*

Thinking Outside the Taco

¿Desde when is it *pereza mental* to express oneself in such a rich and innovative way? *Cada idioma es un revoltijo de palabras prestadas, robadas, adoptadas e impuestas a las buenas o a las malas.* Refusing to understand that is the real *pereza mental.*

I happen to speak two languages and use them both, *cómo diablos me de la gana.* What's so lazy-brained about that? I happen to have two legs, but nobody ever accuses me of using both because I'm too *perezoso* to hop around on either one!

As I am neither monolingual nor mono-ped, I use both languages and both legs, *a veces* simultaneously.

Ya es hora to think outside the taco. It's time to stop persecuting Spanglishistas as workers of lingual iniquity. Besides, I think deep down, our fiercest opponents know they need Spanglish. It keeps them in business.

The *Real Academia Española* is currently recruiting thousands of workers to put up wanted posters of me, with a caption beneath reading: "*Se busca violador del castellano.*" And English Only Online keeps a stable of bloggers busily denouncing my every *spanglishismo* with comments such as: "Worse than ebonics, much worse, maybe even twice as bad."

If only my detractors *pudieran ver la luz* and hear the future of Spanglish *como yo lo he escuchado.*

Spanglish *o Muerte*

My fellow Spanglishistas, *tenemos tiempos difíciles* ahead. I may not get there *con ustedes*, because of the price on *mi cabeza.* But I have seen the promised land (Los Angeles). *Y debemos siempre tener presente que* Spanglish may not be high falutin', *pero tiene una dignidad propia* that we must defend *con orgullo.*

Ay pero to be totally honest, I'm a little ambivalent about the whole thing. *Aunque seré un* Spanglish warrior *hasta que muera*, I actually hope *que* Spanglish never goes *completamente* legit. For me what makes it so fun and irresistible *es el mero hecho de que* you're not supposed to do it. If it were totally accepted, *no se gozaría tanto.*

So if you'll excuse me, I hear there's going to be a book burning, *y tengo que ir a buscar* some matches.

TOP TEN SIGNS LATINOS STILL HAVE A LONG WAY TO GO

1. MY SPELLCHECK STILL CHANGING *"BENDITO"* TO "BANDITO."

2. TELEMUNDO STILL NOT INCLUDED ON BASIC CABLE IN PARTS OF THE COUNTRY.

3. REVISED CENSUS CATEGORIES STILL INCLUDE "NON-WHITE SPIC."

4. STILL MORE LATINOS WORKING IN KITCHENS THAN REMODELING THEIR KITCHENS.

5. *CHUPACABRA* SIGHTINGS STILL NOT CONSIDERED FRONT-PAGE NEWS BY THE "NEW YORK POST."

6. HISPANIC FOODS STILL SHARING AISLE WITH OTHER ETHNIC FOODS AT MAJOR SUPERMARKETS.

7. GYPSY KINGS STILL FOUND IN "FLAMINGO" SECTION OF MANY MUSIC STORES.

8. LOU DOBBS ON CNN IS STILL BLAMING *LA RAZA* FOR 9/11 ATTACKS.

9. HISPANIC HERITAGE MONTH STILL ONLY TWO WEEKS LONG.

10. PUERTO RICANS STILL GETTING PAID MEXICAN WAGES.

10

PHONE AND CYBER SPANGLISH *SON MUY*
USER FRIENDLY

Really? *¡No manches, güey!*

—first known mex-text message

Obviously, *yo no soy el único* speaking Spanglish *por teléfono.* Although no exact figure is available, industry officials confirm that the number of conversations handled by telecommunications satellites containing the phrases "*porque* because," "*pero* anyway," "wow, *qué* great!" "seriously, *no es pa' tanto,*" and "*cójelo con* take it easy" is staggering.

Alexander Graham Bell could not have known the extent of his contribution to the *habla,* but it would be only a matter of time after he spoke the words "*Ven acá* Watson, I need you" before his invention became an instrument of unsurpassed Spanglish propagation. Not only do phone systems transmit Spanglish, but an awful lot of Spanglish revolves around the culture of the phone.

Let's get right to some of my favorite examples of phone Spanglish.

CLASSIC PHONE SPANGLISH

"*Llámame pa'trás* after nine *que* I'm running out of minutes."

"When you have a chance, *dame un fonazo.*"

"*Mira,* I'm going to lose you, *porque mi batería está bien* low. So *llámame* on the landline."

"*Léete bien tu* phone bill *que no te vayan a* overcharge."

"I'll call you back *más tardecito.*"

"Can you hear me now? ¿What about now, *me puedes oír?* 'Pérate, wait . . . ¿y now?"

"I've been calling all day. *No me gusta nadita que tu* phone *esté* off."

"*Voy a tener que ponerme en el* do-not-call list. *Porque esos* telemarketers *siempre están fastidiando.*"

"I know you're there. *Así que* pick up the phone. *Se me olvidó decirte algo.*"

"Hello. ¿*Línea suicida? No me vayas a poner en* hold . . . ¡*Maldito sea! Eso está* so messed up."

"*Favor deje su mensaje* and we will call you back as soon as probable."

Cyber Spanglishistas

Lucky for Spanglish, the Internet came along when it did. English plus Spanish plus instant global distribution equals some pretty *habla*-riffic conditions.

Pero dado que Spanglish is still *en un* primarily spoken stage, *estos co-fenómenos* have an even closer and more dynamic partnership than that. Why? *Porque* because *la informalidad irresistible del* Internet *tiene a* everybody online *escribiendo* the way they actually talk!

Spit it out onto the screen the way it would come out of your mouth and, *sin deliberaciones*, hit "send." That's the mentality *del cyber-espacio, ¿verdad?* Well, the same with Spanglish. *Se habla* exactly *como* it comes out, *y das* it. So the two really are perfectly *matcheados*.

¡LOL!

Además, hay que tener presente el demographic timing. You've got the information age coming of age *justo cuando* the Latino population *de los Estados Unidos está* marching toward *un* census-tipping 40 million. *Esta* convergence *histórica* has unleashed legions of cyber-spanglishistas to take their fledgling *idioma* to the next level.

Suddenly everyday Spanglish-sapiens are reading and writing Spanglish—*emaileando, blogueando, posteando, chateando*, etc.—in a major way. And it looks the way it sounds. *¡Imagínate!* The beautifully blasphemous *abominaciones* that had exclusively been music to our Spanglish ears *ahora también son un* feast *para nuestros* eager *ojos*. Before *el* Internet, *la* web, *la* red, or whatever *lo quieras llamar*, it was rare to read Spanglish, *y hasta más raro* to be *escribiéndolo* yourself.

Today, *todo el mundo's* doing it. *Y el mero acto de estar* writing *en un* mix like that, *va codeando el* Spanglish *más profundamente* into the individual and collective consciousness. The physicality of typing it, *aunque* not as spontaneous *como estarlo hablando*, makes it more real, *más* undeniable. *Deja un*

Spanglish footprint *mucho más impactante*. There's actual evidence now that you can *forwardear* to annoy your friends!

Moreover, the Internet, *por sí mismo*, engenders a completely deregulated *subcultura lingüística* where new *palabritas* are coined faster than even online dictionaries can keep up, where *connotaciones* are *constantemente* in flux, *y el* slang *abunda*.

No wonder the *habla* thrives there. ¡LOL! It's a safe, anything-goes haven, *posibilitando el libre desarrollo del* Spanglish *sin inhibiciones* on an unprecedented scale.

La Web *Mundial*

Devotees of the *habla* are communicating with one another, extending, experimenting with, *fortaleciendo*, and standardizing *el* language as they go, via popular usage and abusage. And this is going on in all the world's Spanglish-speaking countries, *no sólo* in the United States.

La Web *mundial* has even proved to be a lifeline to the underground Spanglish movement in Spain, where lately *se oyen rumores* of bringing back the Inquisition to deal with the Spanglish *amenaza*. It's officially considered so vulgar there that pornography on the Internet is of no concern on the Iberian Peninsula so long as there's no Spanglish text or audio tainting the smut. *Películas* rated "Spanglish" can't even be shown in X-rated theaters. Debbie can do Madrid all she wants, *pero está* totally *prohibido de que hable el* Spanglish!

However, no Inquisition stands a chance against the digitized Spanglish insurgency. *Resistencia* is truly futile when it comes to the vast, ever-growing lexicon of Web-related terminology that happens to be *casi* entirely *en inglés*.

Hasta los mejores Spanish equivalents *suenan* labored, *muy forzados* and inorganic to the context. By which, *quiero decir*, phony. It would seem disingenuous to say you're "*platicando*" *en un* "chat" room, *cuando se siente* so much more natural and direct and just plain honest to say *chateando*.

In France, the word "e-mail" was officially banned by Le Ministry of Lost Causes, *a través de una decisión muy polémica*, and replaced by the much more French-sounding "*baguette electronique.*" *Pero* it just doesn't sound the same.

Internetñol

In the online context, the terminology isn't even normal English anymore. *Ya se podría considerar un* Internet-ease. Spanglish *en este sentido* is assimilating new Internet-specific connotations into Spanish for the sake of clarity. You could easily call it *Internetñol*.

Shockingly immediate access *por cientos de millones de* users around the world to all these freshly minted *términos* means there's no time for slow assimilation by other languages. *La jerga* sinks in, as is, *antes de que* any translation *sea posible*. And belated translations seem awkward and artificial because there's already a globally accepted word attached to the concept.

En algunos casos, Spanglish can get ahead of the technology. So far, during the writing of this book, the word *Spanglish* has come up wrong 37,826,710 times on my spellcheck. Meanwhile, there's already a word for spellcheck in Spanglish: *spellchequear*. Bill Gates really needs to *updatear sus* databases with a little Spanglish, *porque ya* I'm getting tired *de todos esos* squiggly lines *rojos* popping up *cada santo momento*. Please, *Señor* Gates, don't be such a *webón, ¿OK? Arréglelo* on your end, *que no son* typos *de mi parte! Estoy* writing *así* on purpose.

Take a word like "software." This one is so elemental that even the draconian *Real Academia Española* had to make a concession and accept it grudgingly as "non-taboo." *Pero*, I mean, c'mon, you have to use it! The Spanish equivalent is just too much of a mouthful: "*conjunto de programas, instrucciones, y reglas para ejecutar ciertas tareas en una computadora u ordenador.*" But *con decir* "software," you'll add years to your life.

Now, granted, once you accept software, *todos los* bets *están* off. Before you know it, you get "software *bundleado con el* mother." I wouldn't even know what that means in straight English, but it does illustrate the point that the lingo becomes something unto itself.

¡Googleamos!

Every time we use phrases like "*hacer un* cut *y* paste," or "*deletear un* memo," or "*cambiar el* printer cartridge," or "*nuestros sistemas están* down," or "*¡maldito* spam!*" not only are we reinforcing Spanglish fundamentals, *estamos promocionando el* interface *lingüístico del inglés y el español* around the world.

On a day-to-day basis, I get reminders of just how much fun people are having out there with online Spanglish. I just got *un* e-mail, entirely *en* English except for the closing, which read: "*Hasta lu*-ater, Nicky." And a certain bigwig at HBO, who apparently is a big fan of mine and the *habla*, recently *me emailió* after a live show to say, "It was nice to meet you face to '*cara.*'"

Pero quizás, en fin, success of the *habla* online really comes down to the fact that some *joyas* of the *léxico cibernético* are just too good for any self-respecting Spanglishista to pass up. Like the word "google." *Como tiburones* sensing blood *en el agua*, we move in to conjugate English into Spanglish mercilessly. "*Yo googleo, tú googleas, él googlea, ella googlea, ellos googlean, nosotros googleamos . . .*"

The Internet, *sin lugar a dudas,* feeds the Spanglish beast.

TOP TEN SPANGLISH E-MAIL ADDRESSES

1. salsaholic@latinaguanabi.com

2. bigpapi@chiquitabanana.org

3. unemployed@cojelocontakeiteasy.net

4. elpendejojr@thewhitehouse.gov

5. delotroway@brokebacklatinos.com

6. lachismosa@juicydeveras.net

7. fatcharlie@cuchifritocorp.org

8. comoquewhy@porquebecause.com

9. tremendo.coolant@irischacon.edu

10. toosexyformyguayabera@aol.com

11

BIENVENIDOS AL
NEW SPANGLISH ORDER

**I'm turning 30 but don't want to admit it.
So I'm calling it my *doble quinceañera*.**

—my friend Linda, who's actually turning 35

It's only a matter of time before a big huge Spanglish asteroid comes along and completely knocks life as we Americans know it off its monolingual axis. *Hasta pudiera ser que* the sacred text *en tus manos* does the trick. *Vamos a ver*. In the meantime, you can enjoy *los fuegos artificiales* as the media universe *se ilumina* with a constant *bombardeo* of little Spanglish meteorites entering *la atmósfera* mainstream.

Telemundo Nation

"*Estamos tocando* back to back, bumper to bumper, *todas tus favoritas aquí en* Latino Mix," rattles off an FM radio DJ in Los Angeles. "Hey, *mucho* take it easy, OK," *dice* Jack Black *en su película* "Nacho Libre." "*¡Que Vivan Los*

Bears*!"* screams a frontpage newspaper headline *en* Chicago. "What's it gonna be, José, *¿trato* or *no trato?"* asks *el animador* Howie Mandel *en su* game show "Deal or No Deal." "Get the Whole *Enchilada* for Next to *Nada"* promises *un* advertising *de* high-speed internet. "Who died and left you *jefe?" se queja* a trendy T-shirt.

This Telemundo-ization of the non-Spanish-speaking *mundo,* with the vast media market of the United States as its transformational hub, knows no bounds. *Mira, inclusive en los* bumper stickers, *hoy en día,* there's no escaping Spanglish. I was driving down *el* freeway, *hace poco,* when I noticed this one: "My other car *es una porquería también."* And it was on a Rolls Royce, OK.

El pop-cultural graffiti *está en la* wall: *Bienvenidos al* New Spanglish Order. Sure, the vanguard of the order is the Internet, where millions of faithful Spanglishistas are *googleando* the hours away right now. But even the old-school printed word reflects the shift *con un chorro inagotable de* bestsellers, such as "I'm OK, You're a *Pendejo,"* which made publishing history *siendo el primer libro* to ever be selected by both the Oprah and Cristina book clubs!

All the *Verdad* That's Fit for the Masses

Mass communication is massively on board with the *habla,* embracing, reflecting, and fueling Spanglish in ways *que nuestros* bilingual forefathers *nunca se pudieran haber imaginado.* I am personally launching a new network broadcasting nothing but movies dubbed into Spanglish, and I'll do all the translations myself. On the *Porque* Because Channel, *vas a poder* enjoy all your favorite stars de Hollywood *en un* whole new way.

Jack Nicholson in "A Few Good Men": You want *la verdad?* You can't handle *la verdad!*

Bette Davis in "All About Eve": *Abróchense los* seatbelts *porque* it's going to be *una noche muy* bumpy.

Marlon Brando in "The Godfather": *Te voy hacer un* offer *que no vas a poder* refuse.

Robert De Niro in "Raging Bull": *¿Te echaste un polvo con* my wife? *¿Te echaste un polvo con* my wife?

Clint Eastwood in "Dirty Harry": *Pero como este es un* .44 Magnum, *el* handgun *más poderosa del mundo* and would blow your *cabeza* clean off, *tienes que* ask yourself a question. "*¿Me siento* lucky?" *Pues,* do you, punk?

Jake Gyllenhaal in "Brokeback Mountain" *(la de los* cowboys *del otro* way): I wish *que yo pudiera* quit you, *puto.*

Clark Gable in "Gone with the Wind": Frankly my dear, *a mí no me importa un carajo.*

Yo Quiero My Spanglish TV

Television is supremely suited to Spanglish. So I also have *un* show *de* reality *en* development, *que se llama* "*Suegras* Survivor," in which an unlucky contestant *tiene que sobrevivir* on an island *con cinco* prospective mothers-in-law, marrying *la hija de la suegra* he can't stand the least. *Como regalo de boda,* the show picks up the tab for an all-expense-paid honeymoon *para tres.*

By the way, I have an insider secret for you. *¿Quieres saberlo?* OK, well, you know that guy, César Millán, *el* dog whisperer, *que tiene ese programa* on TV, where he performs some sort of doggy *brujería* on *perros salvajes* until they change *milagrosamente* from like Cujo to Lassie? *Pues*, here's how he does it. During *los* commercial breaks, he scares them straight in Spanglish.

He tells the pooch, "*Mira, pórtate bien*, because otherwise *entonces sí*. I'll ship you to Korea, *donde vas a terminar como un* Snoopy burger. *¿Entiendes, Mister Doggy? Ahora*, when the cameras come back on, *atrévete a morderme* if you think *que estoy* kidding."

Of course there's only one undisputed starlet of Spanglish American television. Far more subversive than the Teletubbies, way more marketable than Barney, able to speak English and Spanish in a single sentence … It's the "Let's go! *Vámonos!*" girl herself, Dora the Explorer!

She's like the animated reincarnation of César Chávez in the body of Shirley Temple, *demasiada* cute and down with *la causa*. Even by just minimally sprinkling her English with Spanish, she is singlehandedly (with the help of Boots, her *mono loco*) doing more to boost Spanglish literacy in preschoolers than any other *chica de la pantalla chica*.

In live-action TV, *tenemos el* hit "Ugly Betty," *producido por* Salma Hayek. Salma also produced the movie "Frida," as she seems to like offsetting her own stunning *hermosura* by backing projects about the *belleza*-challenged. It's kind of like Donald Trump producing a revival of the musical "Hair." *Pero* anyway, "Ugly Betty" originally *alcanzó unos* ratings *fenomenales* in Latin America under the title "*Betty La Fea*," which if translated literally would be "Betty the Ugly," and I think it sounds a little more *distinguido* somehow. Salma decided to do an English version of it.

It bears pointing out that the title itself, referring blatantly to the main female character as ugly, is a crossover sensibility, because on Spanish TV and in Spanish-speaking culture (at least in my family), it is very common for a person to be nicknamed according to whatever is most obviously unflattering about them.

Por lo tanto, one of Spanish television's most popular talk shows, hosted by Univisión's beloved Raúl de Molina *y* Lili Estefan, is called "El Gordo y La Flaca," in honor of their celebrated weight differential. It's not considered politically incorrect: simply an honest way to identify someone so that there's no mistaking *de quién estás hablando*. It's just the way we do.

I once dated a woman from Phoenix, *por ejemplo*, who was endowed with *una* extremely large nose. I mean *pero* huge. And my family automatically renamed her "*La narizona de* Arizona." Which, incidentally, is what I'm calling a new crossover *novela* I'm creating for Showtime about a Latina Cyrano de Bergerac–type character from Barstow.

Los Spawn *de* Betty

Crossover programming *no es nada nuevo*. What's new is the direction. Usually it's the U.S. shows that get revamped into *versiones latinoamericanas en español*, like "*Cien Mexicanos Dijeron*," which was based on "Family Feud." And, of course, iconic American television shows *siempre han sido* dubbed into Spanish for broadcast *en latinoamérica*, fulfilling the imperialist Yankee entertainment industry's role in Manifest Destiny, according to *algunos* disgruntled culture war experts. *Y bueno, visto* in that light, "Ugly Betty" is nothing less than "Dallas" blowback. Even in the middle of military coups and economic contretemps, *nuestros vecinos* to the south still stopped to watch the famous "*¿Quién fusiló a* JR*?*" cliffhanger!

Pero anyway, the "*Betty La Fea*" franchise continues to be so popular in

Latin America that its children are still being spawned. Apparently inexhaustible, new titles like "*La Fea Más Bella,*" "*Fea Pero Fea,*" "*Más Fea Que Nunca,*" "*Híjole Qué Fea,*" and "*La Fea de* Outer Space," appear every season. *Así que* don't be surprised *cuando* the American version turns out its own refried *feas* spinoffs: "Hideous Betty," "Desperate Ugly Housewives," "CSI: Uglyville," and "Charlie's *Feas.*"

The Walter Gap

This bridging between the English and Spanish television worlds represents a narrowing of what I call "the Walter Gap." The most trusted broadcast personality ever in the United States is Walter Cronkite, a legend of journalistic integrity, who ended every show with his catchphrase, "And that's the way it is."

The most trusted broadcast personality ever on Spanish television is Walter Mercado, an astrologer in the style of a Latino Liberace, flamboyantly bedecked in a sparkling rhinestone outfit with matching cape. He still ends every appearance with, "*Y que reciban de mí siempre, mucho, mucho, mucho* [stares into the camera] *¡AMORRRRRRRR!*"

But I'll tell you something. I never go a day without consulting Mercado's zodiac predictions because Walter *nunca falla.* The dude is right 99 percent of the time. And while Cronkite retired long ago, Mercado's cult following grows larger every day, and he somehow always looks *quince años más joven* than the last time *que te fijaste.*

Among Latino *televidentes,* Mercado is, by far, guilty pleasure *número uno.*

He's over-the-top in the way only Latinos can be. Which is to say, *exagerado.* And you'd think someone with that kind of wardrobe in his closet couldn't possibly still be in the closet himself, *sin embargo*, he's never publicly acknowledged the obvious. But *el* issue *de sus preferencias íntimas* only adds to the fun and his fans' fascination.

Inexplicably, he recently got hitched to his female assistant, *una rubia*. To which my mother responded, "To a woman? *¿Y a quién él está* trying to fool?*"

But, and *aquí está la cosa*, Walter Mercado doesn't appear on Spanish TV in some Miss Cleo–type infomercial. He's a member of the news team, just like Cronkite was. The news anchors on "*Primer Impacto*" actually cut to him right after the hard headlines. "So far at the crash site there are twenty confirmed fatalities. . . . *Y ahora nos vamos con Walter.*" It's just taken for granted by his *noticiero* colleagues and faithful viewers alike as ludicrously normal.

However, as concepts are now being imported from Spanish-language television to America's networks, and newsrooms in America embrace entertainment ever more desperately, can a Walter Mercado figure on an English-language news show be far behind?

I'd like to broker a deal in which Cronkite comes out of retirement to co-anchor a news program with Mercado. Or, even better, where they trade catch phrases! Imagine Cronkite, signing off in that stentorian voice, " . . . *mucho, mucho, mucho ¡AMORRRRRRRR!*"

And *Cerveza* for My Horses

What about Spanglish *música*, you ask?

Well, the *reggaetoneros* have got the Latino hip-hop market locked up, with Daddy Yankee, Calle 13, Ivy Queen, et al. doing tremendous work *mezclando* English and Spanglish lyrically. Other groups like Yerba Buena are doing interesting blends. Juan Luis Guerra, the world's tallest *merenguero*, recently swept the Latin Grammys with his Spanglish-infused hit *"La llave de mi corazón."*

Plus there's actually a longer history of Spanish mixed into American pop-music lyrics than many people realize, from Doris Day's *"Que será será,* whatever will be will be," to Beck's not quite as cheery, *"Yo soy un perdedor.* I'm a loser baby. So why don't you kill me."

Pero . . . se me ocurre, que the real growth potential in Spanglish music *todavía está* totally untapped.

Every day there are bilingual radio formats popping up all over the Hispanic heartland, in places *como* Tenessee *y* Virginia, Oklahoma *y* Mississippi, *tú sabes.* And they are going to need music that speaks to the merging of cultures in those regions.

So I have been *muy* busy in the recording studio, picking up where Willie Nelson and Julio Iglesias left off with "To All the Girls I've Loved Before." That's right, I am putting together a definitive compilation of the best *canciones* country of all time, *cantadas por primera vez en* Spanglish (*con un poquito de* twang).

Actually, I'm not in the recording studio yet. But I was out doing crossover karaoke last night and delivered *una interpretación* amazing *de* "Mi Achy-Breaky *Corazón,"* which brought down the house, all two *borrachos* at the bar. But I know I'm onto something and have e-mailed Garth Brooks and Shakira, *a ver si quieren cantar* backup for me on the project.

Kentucky Fried *Comerciales*

And if your company *tiene cualquier cosa* at all to sell the masses *en este nuevo* media environment, your brand better be *habla*-relevant. So I'm hearing a lot of Spanglish advertising now, as the "we get you" marketing scramble unleashes an assault of bilingual slogans:

> *"La nueva* **Variety Bucket** *de* **Kentucky Fried Chicken.**
> *Cada pedacito de pollo frito está* **finger-lickin'** *delicioso. "*

Whatever your needs, *puedes estar muy seguro que* there's a Spanglish marketing team *brainstormeando* a pitch just for you.

Your *pantalones* don't fit you anymore? "*Déjame recomendarte el* plan *de* Slimfast, *que* I tried it, *¡y perdí un montón!*" Sending that *quinceañera* gift to *Jalisco*? "*Cuando* it absolutely positively *tiene que llegar* overnight, *puedes trostear a* FedEx." Hair needs to be tamed? "*Prueba el champú de* Frizz Ease *para tu cabello. ¡Porque basta ya con el maldito* frizz*!*" Time for a cell phone upgrade? "Singular Wireless. *Ahora con* push to talk." Want to replace your governor with an Austrian bodybuilding movie star? "*Hasta la vista*, baby!"

Es más, the *habla* gives advertisers *un* unfair advantage. Spanglish consumers are so vulnerable to slogans *en su idioma* that many are tempted to buy things they have absolutely no use for. Case in point: "Always Ultra Panty Guards. *Ninguna otra ultra* protects you *como* Always!" Being a man, I have no use for this product. But when I hear that commercial, *te lo juro,* I feel the urge to run out and get me a box.

It's impossible to overestimate the reach of a trend that now includes Spanglish commercials advertising Spanglish products for the average José. The Miller Brewing Company recently launched a campaign touting its new "*Beerveza*." Get it? It's a beer-*cerveza* hybrid, tweaked with a hint of salt and lime to reference the taste of a Mexican *michelada.* And it's being sold as "*Muy* refreshing!"

Un Tremendo Coolant

Nailing a commercial message with an effectively compelling mix of English and Spanish, however, requires not only exceptional creativity, but the right spokesperson. Thus I would like to nominate my choice for the first inductee into the Spanglish Advertising *Sala de Fama*.

Really, only one person *se merece este* honor. I'm talking about the woman who so unforgettably put the *culo* in the word "coolant." Notorious for her ample posterior charms, singer Iris Chacón starred in a commercial that aired in Puerto Rico back in 1982 and that I never get tired of watching on YouTube. If you haven't seen it, *hazte un* favor and go check it out right now. You'll thank me *tan pronto que termines de reírte*, which may be a few days later.

Playing on the fact that *culo*—colloquial Spanish for "ass," sounds very close to the English word "coolant," especially when pronounced with a Puerto Rican accent, Iris boosted sales of Amalie Engine Coolant by strategically shaking her incomparable *bon bon* to full effect.

Let me put the power of this image in perspective for you. Compared to Iris Chacón, J.Lo's ass is anorexic. We're talking about the real deal here, not a lightweight version designed for export to the mainland. This was genuine island-grown, *cuchifrito*-fed, free-range, Caribbean *culo*.

The legendary commercial features Iris as herself, pulling up and screeching to a stop in a black Corvette, *justo a tiempo* to help a poor fat schlub whose radiator has overheated. "*Ay bendito*," she says, asking what happened, as she gets out in a leopard print bodysuit, cut extra high and wide in the rear to suit her body.

Bending over to get a bottle of the coolant *de calidad* from inside her car, she explains that when it comes to "coolants," she knows *de lo que está* talking about. (Puerto Rican humor is very subtle that way.)

And then, instead of a close-up, the camera actually has to zoom out to get her whole *culo* into the frame. With innuendo rising as thick as the steam from the radiator, Iris saves the day, practically purring, "*Yo tengo un trrrremendo* coolant . . . *Y de* coolant, *yo sí sé.*"

Yes, it certainly was a pioneering performance *en la historia del* Spanglish. And there have been countless others since, as when Rosie O'Donnell introduced Marc Anthony at the Grammy's with these memorable words: "*Su música me encanta en mi corazón. Lo amo mucho. Quiero* Taco Bell. *Mi amiga,* Marc Anthony!"

Refried *Futuro*

Y el futuro está looming, literally, overhead. I was stopped at a traffic light in Hollywood, *esperando que la luz su pusiera* green, *y de repente* I looked up and saw *un enorme* billboard, *casi el tamaño de un* two-story building. Morning radio personality Piolín, grinning wide and giving an enthusiastic *dos* thumbs up, *aparece* against the colors *de una bandera mexicana* in the background.

Off in the upper lefthand corner is a cheeky phonetic English translation of the Spanish for "refried beans." The translation reads: "Free hole is reef free toes: *frijoles refritos.*" Another line, just below, boldly announces that he has the number one show *en el país.* Then, anchoring the entire display of raw *raza*-irreverance are the larger-than-life words, "*We espeekinglish tu!!*"

Sin duda, all these little *blipicitos* in the zeitgeist are steadily adding up to a critical mass.

You may not have been aware of the extent of it before. But once you tune in that Spanglish frequency, *olvídate que* it's impossible not to notice it all around you. So turn on your TV, or radio, *ponte a surfear el* Internet, open a newspaper, or simply keep turning *las páginas* of this *comiquísimo* book.

And get your Spanglish on.

TOP TEN SPANGLISH COUNTRY SONGS

1. "*MI* ACHY BREAKY *CORAZÓN*"

2. "*BABALÚ* PEGGY SUE"

3. "STAND BY YOUR *MUJERIEGO*"

4. "*EL DIABLO SE FUE* DOWN TO GEORGIA"

5. "*YO SOY UNA* REDNECK *CHICA*"

6. "*BÉSAME MUCHO* AND BEER FOR MY HORSES"

7. "DEPORT ME TO HOME DEPOT"

8. "*AMORES* HONKY TONK"

9. "*NO ERES NADA* BUT A HOUND DOG"

10. "TAKE THIS *TRABAJO* AND SHOVE IT"

TOP TEN SPANGLISH ADVERTISING SLOGANS

1. "MELTS *EN TU BOCA*, NOT *EN TUS MANOS.*"

2. "JUST *HAZLO.*"

3. "THE WHOLE *ENCHILDADA* FOR NEXT TO *NADA.*"

4. "*¿ADÓNDE ESTÁ LA* BEEF?"

5. "¿CAN YOU HEAR ME *AHORA?*"

6. "PLOP PLOP, FIZZ FIZZ, *¡AY QUÉ ALIVIO* IT IS!"

7. "HELP, I'VE FALLEN *Y NO ME PUEDO LEVANTAR!*"

8. "PLEASE, *NO LE HAGAS* SQUEEZE *AL* CHARMIN."

9. "*¡Y DE* COOLANT, *YO SÍ SÉ!*"

10. "*¡CADA PEDACITO DE POLLO FRITO ESTÁ* FINGER-LICKIN' *DELICIOSO!*"

12

THE TAO OF
PORQUE BECAUSE

What is a wrap but a gentrified *burrito*?

—Confucius del Toro

I don't know if you've ever been to New York City, but if not, you must go. Many, including myself, consider it the capital of Spanglish, a mecca of the *habla*. In any case, if you ever make the pilgrimage, you won't be disappointed.

I was in a toy store one day, in Times Square, and witnessed such a precious Spanglish exchange. *Jamás lo olvidaré.*

There was a little girl in the middle of the store pointing to a doll she wanted very badly. It was on a shelf, beyond her reach, and she says, "*Mami, cómpramela, por favor, que está* on sale . . ."

Without skipping a beat, the mother, says, "*Te dije que no.*"

"Why?" the little girl cried out.

"*¿Cómo que* why?*"* the mother snapped back. Then she gave the best answer to any question I've ever heard. "*¡Porque* because*!"*

The phrase "*porque* because" is truly greater than the sum of its *palabras*. It's a Teflon because-that's-the-way-it-is jewel of a comeback for any occasion. *Pues*, no wonder *que es tan* catchy. Say it and you instantly justify *cualquier cosa sin necesidad de* further explanation. Clearly, no parent should leave home without it.

Ay, pero esta frase mágica tiene un sinfín de aplicaciones. It is the universal best answer to all the mysteries of the universe—especially if the mystery seems to defy logic. Go ahead and ask me any question of cultural, personal, or general human nature, *y les mostraré* how those two words never fail. No question is too stupid, either.

OK, I'm ready for you. *Ándale.*

Q: Why does *el chupacabras* only appear to Spanish-speaking people?

A: *Porque* because.

Q: Why do we always dream *que estamos desnudos* in public?

A: *Porque* because.

Q: Why don't bulls win more bullfights?

A: *Porque* because.

Q: Why is the entire country of Argentina on the Atkins diet?

A: *Porque* because.

Q: Why can't I understand Brazilian Spanish?

A: OK, that question is too stupid.

Q: Why?

A: *Porque* because.

Q: Why isn't the Spanish translation for "great white sharks" *tiburones gringos?*

A: *Porque* because.

Q: Why does that Don Francisco guy on *"Sábado Gigante"* get to be surrounded by all those *culo*-licious babes?

A: *Porque* because.

Q: How come I can fly to Puerto Rico on a domestic flight and come back on an international flight?

A: *Porque* because.

Q: Why did the chicken cross the road?

A: *Porque* because.

> Q: *¿Oye güey, por qué los mexicanos decimos güey tanto, güey?*
>
> A: *Porque* because, *güey.*

OK, alright already. I think that's enough, *por ahora. ¿Cómo que* why? *Pues,* I think you know the answer to that.

People *En Español*

Some of the most prominent examples of Spanglish are clearly founded in a deep commitment to *porque*-because philosophy. For instance, as a testament to our new status in this country, *nosotros los latinos hasta tenemos* our own magazine now.

Maybe you've heard of it? Yeah, "People." But not that normal "People." We've got our own version: "People *en Español*." It's the only magazine written in Spanish, for Spanish-speaking people who don't know that the word for "people" in Spanish is *"gente"*!

Why don't they just call it *"Gente"*? Well, *¡porque* because*!* Any other explanation sounds ridiculous: "Oh, because we want them to know it's 'People.' If you call it *'Gente,'* they might not make the connection . . ."

I mean, if you break it down, there are so many insults involved with this concept. To start with, it makes it sound like "people" is some sort of higher state of being. Like that's what you're shooting for on the cultural evolutionary scale. Like "people" are *"gente"* who've made it.

"Someday I want to be a people! But today . . . I'm just a *gente.* God, how long does it take to become a people? I hope it doesn't take as long as becoming a citizen! That can take forever."

13

CHANCLA SURVIVOR:
GROWING UP SPANGLISH

I always thought the *locuras* in my family were specific to my house. Then I moved to Puerto Rico and saw four million people behaving the exact same way. And I realized, I'm not dysfunctional. I'm tropical.

—Bill Santiago, *chancla* survivor

As the Spanglish I grew up with eventually led to this book, *ahora vuelvo a mis raíces*, the source from which I still draw Spanglish strength each and every day, *para terminar con lo que me parece el* perfect ending.

Entonces vamos a shift gears *un poquito* and get personal. *Y cuando digo* personal, I mean *sin pelos en la lengua. Porque mira,* Latinos always put it out there and make fun of it, *sea lo que sea.* No matter what the foible or the tragedy, *lo decimos* like it is *y nos reímos* anyway. *Eso sí, que no somos* repressed!

I'd like to include a little transcript of an actual Spanglish family. *La mía*, of course. *Ya verán como esto pondrá* everything *de lo que hemos estado* talking about into context, *siendo un ejemplo de* Spanglish in action with multiple *hablantes*. As far as I'm concerned, what's going on *en tales ocasiones* is absolutely and *sin duda alguna*, a Spanglish event, because those involved *se entienden a través de* two different languages engaging symbiotically *como un solo sistema de comunicación*.

Pero first you'll need a little background *de cómo* I grew up and to meet *algunos de los* characters *en* my life.

First Born

I don't know about all of you, *pero* I myself was born in New York, like most Puerto Ricans. It's been said I was "born to Puerto Rican immigrants." *Lo cual es* technically untrue, because *los puertorriqueños somos* U.S. citizens. Although, *debo admitirlo*, I did have an uncle who once got deported to the Bronx.

I am the first born of at least four children. And I went to George Washington Elementary School. We were the only Puerto Ricans in that school. And in the school play, I got to play the part of George Washington. *¿Qué les parece?* I was a founding *papi!*

You should have seen me and Martha *bailando salsa* at the inaugural ball *hasta las tantas*. It even made the school newspaper the next day: "Fifth Grader Elected El Presidente. Fiesta Goes On Way Past Bed-Time."

Mi White Castle *Es Tú* White Castle

Back then I ate a lot of White Castles. *De hecho*, I just assumed White Castles was traditional Puerto Rican food, because I pretty much went straight from breast-feeding to White Castle hamburgers. *Así que pensé que tenía que ser comida típica de la cultura.*

My father used to take us constantly *porque había un* White Castle *cerca de su oficina* on Prospect Avenue. *Pero bien sabido era que los* fries *de* McDonald's *eran mejores.* So we would get the burgers at White Castle and then drive over to McDonald's, *para que mi papi pudiera conseguir* the better *papitas* for his children. *Todavía lo recuerdo como* the greatest gesture of parental love, *y estoy seguro de que* people have been recognized as saints for lesser deeds.

You may think I'm *jokeando*, but White Castle played a significant role in my Puerto Rican upbringing. Every year, *para Sanksgibing,* my mother would stuff our turkey with eighty to ninety White Castle hamburgers. *Entonces*, all our friends and neighbors would come over and rave.

"Oh my God, this Puerto Rican stuffing is incredible! Can we have the recipe?"

"Sorry, family secret," *decíamos nosotros*, scrambling to hide all the little square boxes.

Latinos in Space

Now here's a joke I heard. You'll see the reason I'm telling you in just a little bit.

Q. Why were there no Puerto Ricans on "Star Trek"?

A. Because they're lazy in the future too.

You know how I heard that joke? From a Mexican. My girlfriend's brother told it to her over the phone. *Pero él no sabía que ella lo tenía* on speaker phone, and that I was listening. *¡Imagínate!*

But what cracked me up *era que* I used to watch "Star Trek," and Captain Kirk always seemed very Latino to me. *Su* behavior *y su* look, *tú sabes.* He wore those bright-colored shirts and had such over-the-top bravado. *Y tenía siempre su pelo* slicked back. *Además, era bien mujeriego* to boot. *Olvídate,* Kirk *era un* playboy *fuera de serie y levantaba sus mamacitas* all over the universe.

And since all the Latinos I knew at the time *eran puertorriqueños,* as far as I was concerned, Captain Kirk was *boricua* all the way.

There was even an episode called "Space Seed," *en el cual apareció* Ricardo Montalbán, playing the character he later reprised in the movie "Wrath of Khan." Yet even though Montalbán was speaking with a thick Spanish accent, I still thought of Captain Kirk *como el más latino* of the two.

Then one day, there's this commercial that comes on, with the Starship Enterprise in it. And the ship pulls into a drive-thru orbit *alrededor de la tierra* to order White Castles. *Y pensé yo,* "No way!" *Entonces* Captain Kirk *ordenó* like 500 *de esos riquísimos* little square hamburgers for the entire crew, *y que* "to beam up."

And I said to myself, "*¡Mira pa' ya,* Captain Kirk eats White Castles!*" How much more Puerto Rican can you get than that?

Me Llamo Bill

There were four of us boys in the house growing up. My three brothers and I: Billy, Tony, Tierney, and Larry, *en el orden que nacimos*. I know they're not "typical" Puerto Rican names. To which I say: *¿Y qué, so what?*

Look, *como fui el primero*, I got named after my father, William, who was named after his father, Guillermo, which is Spanish for William. *Entonces* Bill *es el apodo de* William *en inglés*. And Mami still calls me Billy, which she still pronounces as "Bee-Lee."

After me, my parents *estaban* free to pick and choose names from *las estrellas del* show business.

My brother Tony was named after *el actor* Anthony Quinn. *Y como si fuera poco*, his middle name is Elvis, after Michael Jackson's ex-wife's dad. My brother Tierney is the most testosterone-driven *de todos nosotros*, even though he was named after a woman, *la actriz* Gene Tierney. *Quizás estará* compensating. My youngest brother, Larry, is named for Lawrence of Arabia. My mother *le encantó esa película*. And *cuando* Larry *era un* baby, *a veces* she would wrap a second diaper up on his head, as a turban.

Not so secretly, though, I often wish *que yo tuviera* a real super Latino name, like Benicio del Toro. You could add "del Toro" to any name and it would instantly sound Latino, no matter how un-Latino it was: Chad del Toro; Captain Kirk del Toro; Scooby Doo del Toro.

Of course, "del Toro" means "of the Bull." So maybe I could tack it onto my initials, and be known as B. S. del Toro. But I'd lose a lot of credibility. "Yeah, don't listen to a thing that guy says. Don't you know? That's B.S. del Toro."

A veces, like at a salsa club, *me presento como* Guillermo, just to make things easier. If I introduce myself as "Bill," the music actually stops. "*¿Cómo que, Biew?*" they ask, implying, "What the hell kind of a Spanish name is that?" It can be pretty jarring, *especialmente porque muchas veces* Spanish-speaking people can't pronounce Bill properly. I get *Biew* a lot. It's sort of a combination of Bill and "eww," as in "*eww ¡qué* disgusting!*"*

I'm toying with the idea of dropping Bill altogether and just going as Santiago. Or Santiago del Toro. Which has a nice ring to it. But I just got a great deal on some new business cards and got ten million made.

Así que I'm sticking with "Biew" *por lo menos hasta que* I run out.

Do You Smell Smoke?

My parents met at Papi's law office in the Bronx. Mami came in one day to have her taxes done. And I am a result of that. *Si no fuera por el* IRS, I wouldn't even be here. So every year *cuando estoy* filling out *mis* taxes, I just figure I really do owe them everything.

Papi *pensó que* Mami *era* such a hotty that he kept making excuses for her to have to keep coming back *un sin número de veces.* "Yes, Miss Valentín, why don't you come again tomorrow. I need to see some more receipts. By the way, *¿A usted le gusta bailar?*"

My mother was a Manhattan beauty queen. *Es más,* in her neighborhood, *se conocía como el pollo de la novena.* She even won *un certamen de belleza,* the "Miss Five Boroughs" beauty pageant. By the way, that's "boroughs," not "*burros.*" And she won the title *después que se casó con mi Papi.* Well, who do you think entered her in the contest? My father wanted a trophy wife, *aunque fuera* retroactively.

Their courtship took place primarily *en las pistas* of the most popular salsa spots *en Nueva York* at the time, *El Caborojeño,* Happy Hill Casino, *Los Panchos, Los Violines,* and *El Palladium.*

When my mom speaks of those places her eyes light up. "*Ay, y ¿qué puertorriqueño que viniera aquí no quería un baile?* That's why I married your father. *Le encantaba* to dance *y me llevaba* every weekend. *Ésa era la recompensa de la gran jornada de la semana. Y tú entrabas* for only three dollars," she'll say, with a shimmy of the shoulders and a shake of the hips, as her syncopated body memories kick in. "*Así fue, hasta que* I got married. *Entonces* no more dancing! *Bueno,* at least for me, *porque tu papá todavía tenía su* night life."

As a confirmed *mujeriego,* Papi never let marriage cramp his bachelor style. Let's just say Papi made Bill Clinton look like an ideal husband. My mother frequently *lamentaba el no haberse casado* with a man as faithful as Bill Clinton. "*Ay, esa* Hillary doesn't know *cómo de* lucky she is, *de haber conseguido un esposo tan fiel y respetuoso.*"

Cada vez que Papi *tenía un* affair, my mother would burn all his clothes, his entire wardrobe, on the front lawn. She'd pile them up, *y le echaba* kerosene. Why she needed kerosene, I don't know, *porque el* polyester *ya era* highly flammable. *Entonces, encendía un fósforo.* And whoosh, it was Bonfire of the Infidelities.

The neighbors would get used to it, *y ni se molestaban en llamar a los bomberos.* "Do you smell smoke?" "Oh, don't worry about it. Mr. Santiago must have a new secretary."

Of course, *esto lo único que hacía era* to make things worse, attracting even more other women to Papi, because he always looked irresistibly *guapo* wearing brand new clothes. Whenever my mother *ya estaba harta,* she'd just fly off to Puerto Rico, taking all us kids along with her. By the time I was six months old, I had racked up millions of frequent *mujeriego* miles.

There was never any effort to try and hide any of this from my brothers and me, either. My mother would bring us into it! She'd find my father's mistress's panties in the car and share her discovery. "Billy, *mira lo que yo encontré en el carro de tu papá. Tenemos que ir a ver a la santera.*"

I would hear my friends' parents saying things like, "Honey, let's not fight in front of the kids." Meanwhile my parents, if they ever felt a good fight coming on, would postpone the bout until we got home from school *para que* we wouldn't miss it.

We'd walk through the door. Mami and Papi would be in their corners. A bell would ring.

And my mother would go nuclear: "*¿Y dónde carajo estabas metido hasta las cuatro de la mañana? ¡Desgraciado, maldito, canalla, sin vergüenza . . . HIJO DE LA GRAN PUTA!*"

Oh, we heard that one a lot. *Hijo de la gran puta.* But we were so young when we were first exposed to the expression *que no fuimos capaces de imaginarnos* that it actually meant *algo tan* awful *como:* "son of the great whore." Honestly, when I was little, it sounded kind of sing-songy to me, like a lullaby. "*Hijo . . . de la gran puuutaaaa. Hiiiiiijoo de la graaaaaaan pu-u-u-taaa . . .*" For years, I couldn't get to sleep without hearing it echoing someplace in the house.

Pero un día, you connect the dots. "Wait a minute, *hijo*, that's my dad. He's the *hijo*. So *la gran puta . . .* What? *¿Mi abuelita?* She's *la Gran Puta?*"

I was shocked. And suddenly it sounded so imperial to me. I could picture my grandmother sitting on a throne: "*Yo soy la Gran Puta.* And your *papi*, he is the *hijo. Hijo de la Gran Puta.* And you Billy, *tú eres el nietecito*, grandson *de la Gran Puta.*"

And yes, we were traumatized by my parents divorce. Because they never got one. Mami hung in there, *tú sabes*. She wasn't about to walk away after investing so much of herself in her family. And there were other reasons. Somehow, *a pesar de sus indiscreciones,* Papi was the best father in the world. And we all, including Mami, loved him immensely (*ropa quemada* notwithstanding).

Plus, *¿quién iba a divorciar a mis padres?* My father was Mami's lawyer. And he was perfectly happy with the situation.

That's *Amor*

Although growing up I never knew my father as a lawyer. *Íbamos a visitarlo a su oficina,* but I never saw him in action during a trial or anything. *Así que,* as far as I was concerned, Papi's only job *era* to make sure *que* nobody ever turned the thermostat up over 32 degrees.

Papi, *bendito,* just didn't believe in turning up the heat. "You have to acclimate, Billy. Just acclimate," he'd say, his breath rising visibly in our living room. And I'd say, "Acclimate?! What, build an igloo? It's warmer outside, where it's below zero."

Not only was he saving money on heat. As long as our teeth were chattering, they weren't chewing. *Por lo tanto,* Papi *también estaba* cutting his grocery bills in half!

So there we were, four little Puerto Rican spiccicles, *frizando* our *culitos* off. And every winter we would actually pray for my father to have more frequent affairs, *para poder calentarnos* by the fire that my mother would inevitably make by setting his wardrobe ablaze *en un incendio de venganza.*

Yet, one day, *mis padres* started getting along. After decades of tribulation, involving many scenes of my mother literally dragging *las mujeres rivales*—out of my father's office, out of his car, or out of some club—by the hair, *a puros gritos*, things calmed down. The Gaza Strip–style animosity and rancor *se esfumó de una manera milagrosa.*

I remember calling home one time *y fue Papi quien contestó el teléfono.* "Guess who's here with me, Billy, *aquí mismo*, next to me, in bed," he said. "You'll never guess." "Who?" I said. "*Tu mamá*," he said.

And I was a little stunned, because they hadn't shared a bedroom, much less a bed, in forever.

"You don't believe me, right?" he said. Then I heard him, off the phone, saying, "See, I told you he wouldn't believe me, Judy. *Toma, dile tú.*" And then my mother got on. "It's true, Billy. *Estoy aquí* next to your father."

After that stunning truce my mother revised her official position on matrimony. "Marriage can be a beautiful thing, Billy," she said. "If you can get through the first 30 years, the rest is easy."

Their reconciliation, *por más demorada que fuera*, came just in time in a way. A few short *añitos después*, Papi was diagnosed with cancer, *pobrecito.* When he woke up from his first operation *para removerle el tumor de su colon*, we were all there. In a strained voice, still barely able to open his eyes, *nos hizo reír* with his first words. "I'll be back," he said, hoarsely mimicking *el valor de un* action hero. And he was back with us for a few years more, *con Mami a su lado, cuidándolo hasta lo último.*

That day *en el* ICU *del* Veterans Hospital in the Bronx, *cuando Papi se despertó* with his typical incorrigible charm, the mood lightened. And my mother, *acariciándole su frente*, immediately started poking fun at him, through her grateful tears.

"*Para que tú veas*," she said, compelled to point out that she was gladly there for him *como su esposa*, although as her husband he didn't deserve it. "*Después de las tantas que tú me has hecho sufrir*, I'm still here."

My father smiled, glancing at her, then over at me, and said, "Yeah. It's a real love story."

Everybody Loves Santiago

In a meeting with a producer once, I got an earful of one man's prepackaged idea for a sitcom concept that might be built *alrededor de* Bill Santiago. "OK, so you're Puerto Rican, right?" he said. "So we do a show about you growing up on welfare in the projects in a broken home with half a dozen brothers and sisters, all from different dads."

I said, "Whoa, wait, *'perate un segundito*, hold on. First of all, we weren't on welfare. My father was a lawyer."

"Lawyer," he said, disappointed. "That's not funny."

"And my mom was a school bus driver."

"OK, well, a school bus driver, that's funny," he said, perking up *otra vez*. "So we do a show about you riding around with your mom on the school bus, through the worst neighborhoods in the city, picking up little bad-ass Puerto Rican kids. And the bus isn't just yellow, it's welfare-cheese yellow . . . "

La verdad del caso es que we did eat a lot of welfare cheese at *Casa Santiago*. But it wasn't because *nosotros estábamos* on welfare. *Era que* some of Papi's clients were on welfare *y se les hacía difícil pagar* cash for his legal services. *Como no tenían dinero*, he let them pay with whatever they could. *Muchas veces* it was blocks of welfare cheese, *lo cual funcionaba* as a sort of Puerto Rican wampum at my father's office. It was a payment plan *que* Papi *ofrecía con mucho gusto*, as a Bronx courtesy.

Cuánto queso was due, *se basaba* on what specific legal service my father was providing. *Por ejemplo*, handling *un divorcio* might be worth three blocks of welfare cheese. *Un caso de inmigración* might be more in the range of five blocks. Defending you in a felony case where you were clearly *culpable* might set you back *diez bloques del queso "Tío Sam."*

As a result, our refrigerator at home was always full of the stuff, which came in loaf-sized cardboard boxes. We could have easily built a whole new house *con todo el* welfare cheese *que nos comimos* during our childhood. We had it on Ritz crackers, in grilled welfare-cheese sandwiches, layered into lasagna, melted onto pizza. *Y a mí siempre me encantaba* to slip a *pedazo* under the little square bun, for an extra cheesy White Castle cheeseburger. It's the closest I've ever come to dropping acid.

And if you've never tried this highly prized black market dairy product yourself, *no tienes una idea de lo que te estás* missing. A thick slice of this delicious and nutritious government snack will beat the hell out of any overpriced Brie you've ever tasted, and make you wonder why anyone would want to live above the poverty level. *Así de delicioso es.*

Cuando one day I get *mi propio* sitcom *en la televisión*, I will absolutely insist that the main character on "Everybody Loves Santiago" have a secret weakness for *Le Fromage du* Welfare.

Plus, I must beg to differ on the opinion that my father being a lawyer was not funny.

Papi's Payphone

My father could call anywhere in the world from the payphone in his office *con una sola* quarter.

It was a big black city payphone—with the coin box missing. *Se le había quitado a propósito,* so that you could use the same quarter over and over *para hacer una llamada.* Papi's *amigo* Pisini, a mechanic, all-around fix-it man, and Bronx *raquetero* (in the best sense of that word) had hooked up my father, the lawyer, *con este muy especial* and not-so-legal communication device.

Such a phone had to be kept on the down low, *tú sabes.* When he wanted to use it, my father closed the blinds. *Y como era una operación tan pero tan* hush-hush, Papi *siempre* waited *hasta que* there were no clients left in his office. *Entonces ponía un* sign *en la ventana con* scotch tape *que decía* "Be Back Soon," *y cerraba la puerta con llave.*

Then he'd pull out the phone from its hiding place in the bottom drawer of one his large filing cabinets and prop it up *encima de su escritorio.* Next, *conectaba los* wires *a través de unos* roach clips to the regular phone company line *corriendo* along the baseboard, where Pisini had stripped away the plastic coating *para tener* easy access.

Immediately *tenías un* dial tone *y estabas* good to go. *Marcabas el número,* long distance, *por supuesto.* And *la operadora* would get on the line and tell you *cuánto dinero le tenías que echar.* You'd put a quarter in the slot. *Entonces* quickly swing your hand down, and *la metías* palm up, *dentro del* hollow space where the coin box used to be. *Bueno, y la misma* quarter *que acababas de depositar* plopped into your hand, *emocionándote con el* rush of beating the system.

Pero whenever Papi called me on this phone while I was living in Puerto Rico, the operator was constantly interrupting, *pidiendo más dinero.* "Please deposit another 75 cents for the next minute," she would say.

And I could barely keep myself from laughing at how much Papi would get into the charade. "Yes, operator. Hold on," he'd say, pretending that he was scrounging for change. "I know I had some more here in my pocket. Let me just dig a little. Nope, nope. Just a second. Oh, here's a quarter. Let me put it in. I'm putting it in. I put it in. Did you get that quarter, operator? Good. So Billy, where were we?"

Since back then *llamadas de* long distance *costaban* a pretty penny, Papi *consideraba que su* free pay phone *era su* golden goose. *Es más*, he told me once that he paid off *la hipoteca* and put us through college on the savings. That's a family secret though. *No se lo vayan a decir a* nobody.

I'll Be Home for *Sanksgibing*

The legend of Papi's payphone is one of the many stories that get told over and over whenever my family *se reúne.* Which is why I never miss *el Día del Pavo-chón.*

These days we always do Thanksgiving at my Titi Norma's house. I say "house" *pero es su apartamento,* which is conveniently located *en el mismo* building *donde* my grandmother lives.

Mama (that's what we call *mi abuelita* on my mother's side, not to be confused with *la gran puta* on my father's side, which is a joke, OK?) lives on the 31st floor. Titi Norma is on the 9th. The building's in Hell's Kitchen over on 10th Ave. And, *mis queridos lectores,* you're all invited. Make a left when you get out of the elevator.

I love soaking up the whole *Sanskgibing* experience *desde el momento que* Titi greets me at the door.

"*Oye* Billy, *pero* wow, look at those new shoes. *¡Parece que esos* jokes *están dejando chavos!*" she'll say with a hug, as my eyes adjust to her new hair color. "How do you like it? *Dicen que las* blondes have more fun, right?"

I try to be there by 2 P.M., because that's when Mama starts making the rice. *Y pues,* one of my life's greatest ambitions is to learn *como cocinar un buen arroz puertorriqueño.* Puerto Rican rice, whether it's *con gandules* or *con habichuelas* or *pollo*, or *cualquier manera que* you want to make it, is extremely tricky to get right.

But my grandmother, *quien acaba de cumplir sus* 90 *añitos*, tries teaching me, the way Yoda would guide a young Jedi. Standing about as tall as Yoda herself, she patiently indulges my eager but clumsy attempts. "*Voltéalo y pruébalo de sal*," Mama says, instructing me on the basic turning and tasting technique, as the water starts to boil away, releasing the soul-nourishing aroma of *sofrito* into the air. "*El arroz de abajo tiene que quedar encima.*"

There's no recipe. No measurements. And whenever I ask for specifics, she says, "*Yo nunca mido. Ya más o menos yo sé,*" essentially *diciéndome que* I just have to *trostear* the Force.

So I follow as best I can, *pendiente de todo que* she puts into the bubbling *olla*, that iconic cast iron pot in which she makes magic happen every time, *a fuego lento*. I watch the onions go in and the peppers and the *recaíto* and the *ajo* and the rice and the *gandules* and little pieces of *jamón* and the *aceite* and *un chin de achiote*, for color. *Pero entonces* the second I turn away, *ella*, she pulls a fast one on me.

I sense her tossing something else in there, behind my back. I hear it go plop. I turn around in time to see the little splash. "What was that?" I ask her. "*Nada*," she says, *disimulando*. But I am sure there's some secret ingredient *que ella le está agregando* when I'm not looking! *Es que ella*, she just doesn't want anybody else ever to make it as good as she does. Not even me! "Mama, *¿qué fue eso que le acabas de echar al arroz?*" I ask again. "*Nada*," she repeats, smiling mischievously.

We don't all eat at the same time. *La mesa del comedor es muy pequeña.* And it's impossible to get my family to all show up *a la misma hora*, anyway. So we eat in shifts. The turkey and the *lechón* and *el* stuffing *y el* punkin' pie and the cranberry sauce (from a can *por supuesto*) *y el arroz* (I helped) and the *pasteles* all keep coming as different people keep sitting down for their turn.

But the *pasteles se acaban* pretty quick. They might as well be filled with the best caviar in the world, because that's how *nosotros los puertorriqueños* react to *pasteles*. We go nuts for the *pasteles*. If the United States had ever tried to take away our *pasteles*, Puerto Rico would not be a U.S. possession today. You can have our sovereignty, *pero nuestros pasteles*, never.

Our family gets them "from a lady in the building." This lady is never identified by name, but we've been *outsourceando* the labor-intensive *pasteles* production to her ever since *que se le hizo muy difícil a mi abuelita* a few years ago and nobody else volunteered.

Puerto Rican *pasteles* are kind of like Mexican *tamales* except not. In fact, forget I said that. They're nothing alike. If you haven't tried them, *no tengo tiempo aquí* to get into it. Just make sure you drop by early, *para que puedas probarlos y saborearlos* for yourself. Or put in an order with the lady, *que* she ships worldwide.

The probability of dancing during the evening is high. *Se pone una musiquita.* Usually, we just turn up La Mega 97.9 FM *en la radio.* Push the furniture back a little and go to town. Mami and Titi Norma dust off their moves and *¡Wepa!* put us to shame, while we all try to keep up. *Cuando* these two sisters *empiezan a bailar*, it's a show, *déjame decirte*.

Just FYI: It's gonna get pretty loud, too. *Todo el mundo* will be talking over each other. Kids will be screaming. I have three very loud little cousins, Asia, 11, Enrique, 11, and Amar, 8. Enrique is my cousin Quique's kid. Asia and Amar are my cousin Taisha's kids. *Pero* Taisha *murió* of an overdose a few years ago, *algo demasiado triste*, and Titi Norma has dutifully taken up parental duties. But her grandkids *a veces* are a little more than she can handle.

So guaranteed, you are going to hear the words "Stop it!" no less than five thousand times tonight. They will be followed by auxiliary warnings, ultimatums, and expressions of exasperation, such as: "*¡'Tasen quietos!*" "*¡Basta ya!*" "*¡Les voy a pegar!*" "*¡Qué jodienda!*" and "*¡Dios mío, estos* kids me *están volviendo* crrrrraaaazy!*"

You're not going to hear much from my *abuelito*, though. He's gonna be busy eating, *como si jamás huberia comido* ever before in his life. He just puts his head down and doesn't come up for air, until he finally announces that he has to go to the bathroom. And all night people *van a estar* marveling at how his full head of hair *todavía se ve* jet black, *aunque* he swears *que no se lo pinta.* Oh, and he and my grandmother aren't together. *Se divorciaron* like sixty years ago. *Lo cual tiene que ser* some kind of record for people who still talk to each other.

I think she's extra nice to him *para que se arrepienta*, even though she would never want him *pa'trás.* But she gets a kick out of the fact that he must still find her attractive. Before she goes home to her apartment upstairs, she'll whisper to me, with a little playful smirk, "*Esta noche, él sueña conmigo.*"

My brothers are gonna be there. Tony might be in Paris. But we usually get a three out of four turnout for the *hermanos*, which is pretty good. It's always interesting to see who brings what girlfriend. One year my brother Tierney brought his girlfriend Cara. When he introduced Cara, my grandmother misunderstood and thought Tierney wanted approval for his girlfriend's face. And Mama responded, "*Sí, tiene una cara muy bonita.*"

My father will be missing this Thanksgiving *por segunda vez*, and we'll be missing Papi very much, but we'll try to keep the conversation going, anyway, *para no estar* dwelling on it. Luckily, these holiday get-togethers are when the family's collective sense of humor seems to shine the most.

As more people join in, *la conversación se vuelve más* out of control. And before long, *hay un hilo gracioso que se va formando.* Next thing you know, Titi Norma *está contándonos* a classic story about *su niñez en* Puerto Rico, a tale *quizás* of her first brush with *espiritismo.* Which sparks *una serie divertidísima de comentarios.*

> **Titi Norma:** When I was a little girl, *me hicieron un mal de ojo.* Do you know what that is, evil eye? *¿Mal de ojo?* Anyway, *entonces,* this lady, *una curandera,* told Mama to get *una palomita blanca pa' que* she could cure me. Because I got very sick *con una fiebre* that wouldn't go down.

> **My Brother Larry:** And it had to be white.

> **Titi Norma:** Right, and then Mama got one from a neighbor and *la curandera* took *la paloma viva y la partió* in half.

> **My Brother Larry:** No!

> **My Brother Tierney:** While it was still alive?

> **Titi Norma:** Yes. *Y me pusieron la mitad* with the blood and everything *en el pecho.*

> **My Brother Tierney:** Didn't they have doctors back then?

My Brother Larry: Doctors don't know what to do about *mal de ojos.* You need alternative medicine.

Titi Norma: *Ustedes pueden* make fun, *pero* it's about faith. And I know yous are atheists.

My Brother Tierney: Since when are "wes" atheists?

Titi Norma: Anyway, she put it, *la mitad de la palomita,* on my chest all night, for it could take out what I had.

My Brother Larry: How does that work, exactly?

Titi Norma: I don't know, *pero* I lived. *Se me quitó la fiebre.*

My Mother: *Gracias a Dios, porque* I don't like to cook.

Titi Norma: And I make a good turkey. *Mejor que la* Rachael Ray. Plus, she don't make a *lechón* too. And we have both. *Lo único que* I can't make them in under thirty minutes.

Me: Mami doesn't even like being in the kitchen for five minutes.

My Mother: *Hay gente que* enjoy *la cocina.* Not me.

Titi Norma: So what? That's not her thing. *A tu mamá lo que le gusta son los* dirty jobs. *Le gusta* to be working on her house. *Ella es un capricornio con ascendente en* handyman.

My Mother: Yes. It's true. *Oye,* and you know what? *Me gusta también el tipo ese del* show *de* "Dirty Jobs." *En el* Discovery Channel. *¿Tú has visto ese programa?* I find that man very sexy. *No le dice que "no" a nada.* And I like that. Very masculine. *Es algo así como* John Wayne. *No se ve* wimpy, you know.

Me: Too bad you can't have him at home *ayudándote.*

My Mother: *Sería un hombre ideal,* Mr. Dirty Job, *que a donde-quiera que hay un trabajo difícil,* he goes and does it. *Pero a lo mejor en la casa no hace nada.*

Titi Norma: *Oye* Billy, why don't you get your own reality show?

My Mother: *Pero* no dirty jokes, please.

Titi Norma: Yeah, Billy, remember, you don't have to talk dirty to be famous, *como* Richard Pryor. He made it, *pero él era bien* nasty, *todo* vulgar. And you don't have to be *hablando tan sucio* to make people laugh.

My Mother: And don't make fun of the President. *Acuérdate lo que le pasó a las Chicas Dixie.* Think of your career.

My Little Cousin Enrique: Billy, are you famous?

Me: Not exactly. I'm internationally *desconocido*.

My Mother: Billy, *y ¿adónde vas* on your next trip?

Me: *Para* Seattle.

My Mother: *Cialis?*

My Brother Larry: You're performing in *Cialis?*

Me: Yeah, if I'm not back in four hours call a doctor. Or a *curandera* lady.

(THE LITTLE COUSINS ALL RUN THROUGH SCREAMING)

Titi: *¡Basta ya!* Stop making so much noise! *Qué jodienda.* Thank God *que mañana tengo el* day off. Porque I'm going to have a headache.

My Brother Larry: Titi, you need to domesticate these kids.

Titi Norma: What can I do? I can't be hitting them all the time.

My Mother: *Ya yo los hubiera ahorcado.*

Titi Norma: *Es que se ponen* hyper. When you were kids, weren't you rascals?

My Brother Tierney: We were domesticated.

My Brother Larry: Ma and Pa used to tag team us, like they were wrestlers.

My Mother: *Pero mira cómo* you turned out! *En mi casa* everybody *siempre ha tenido que* behave.

My Brother Larry: Except for the dog.

Me: Yeah, Mami, *ese perro está salvaje.* You should at least teach him how to sit.

My Mother: *Él se sienta cuando le da la gana.*

My Brother Tierney: That's a double standard.

My Mother: *Oye ese perrito* keeps me company. He sleeps with me, *y yo me lo llevo al cementerio* whenever I go. And he misses your father too.

My Grandmother: *Ay* William, *en paz descanse, 'dito. Le hubiera encantado estos pasteles.*

My Mother: *Están buenísimos.*

My Brother Larry: Who made them? Mama, *¿tú hiciste los pasteles?*

Titi Norma: No, we got them from a lady in the building. Asia, *¿vas a comer?*

My Little Cousin Asia: Not yet.

Titi Norma: Not yet? *Pues, ¡quítate de la mesa si no vas a comer,* yet!

My Brother Larry: Asia, do you speak Spanish?

Titi Norma: Yeah, *ella habla más que ninguno. Ella entiende y habla. ¿Verdad que tú hablas español?*

My Little Cousin Asia: Not really.

Titi Norma: *¡No digas eso! Yo les enseño.* I don't know what she's talking about.

My Mother (stroking Asia's hair): Asia *tiene el mismo pelo de su mamá, tan grueso.*

Titi Norma: *Y de su* grandma *también.* You've seen the pictures, right? Of me *con mi pelo negro* down to there?

My Brother Tierney: And the go-go boots. You were always the hot aunt. When I was little I thought you were Cat Woman.

Titi Norma: Those were my wild disco days! *Pero yo no soy la misma* Norma that used to be. *Porque* I'm born again.

My Cousin Quique: (enters) *Buen provecho.*

My Brother Tierney: Speak of the devil.

Titi Norma: *¿Cómo que* devil *ni qué* devil? Quique already gave his life to the Lord. He backslided a little. *Pero* he just got a job!

My Cousin Quique: I had to change seventeen tires today.

Titi Norma: *Está trabajando en un* tow truck, *haciendo* emergency calls.

My Mother: *Pues, un* dirty job!

My Cousin Quique: *Chacho,* and then you get those big vans with the eight lug nuts, fully loaded. I threw my back out.

Titi Norma: But it's a job. *Dios mío, Señor.* Praise the Lord! You see? God is up there *escuchando* and he answered my prayers.

My Grandmother: *Quiro, ¿quieres un poquito del pegao?*

My Cousin Quique: *Si, por favor.* Where's Tony?

Me: Paris.

My Cousin Quique: Gay *Paris!*

My Grandmother: *'Dito. Eso no es nada. Hay muchísima gente del otro* way.

My Mother: Norma, what I would like to know is, is there anything *después que* you die? Another dimension of life, or what's going on? You know? *No sabemos.* No one come and say, "Yes, Judy."

Titi Norma: William is up there. Believe me. *De eso puedes estar segura.* At least I hope it's up there and not in the other place.

My Mother: *Estuvimos casados* forty-two years and ten days.

My Brother Larry: Wow. Can you believe Mama and *abuelito* have been divorced longer than that?

Abuelito: *Tengo que ir al baño.*

My Mother: And your father used to tell me, "I was married to you previously, and I will be married with you again, in the next life." *Y yo le decía,* "No way!" *Decía él,* "I'm going to come for you, Judy." *Y yo le decía,* "No way. Once is enough." *Pero* if he comes for me, yes, I will go.

Titi Norma (*pegando un grito a todo pulmón*): Enrique! Amar! Stop it! Asia—

My Little Cousin Asia: I know. Stop it.

Titi Norma: They wanted to go to the parade this year. *Pero estaba muy frío* so we watched it on TV. Santa Claus was there and some *santaclausitas bailando también*. But we went last year.

My Brother Tierney: Yeah? Do they board up the storefront windows like they do for the Puerto Rican Day Parade?

Mami and Papi Got My Back

Yeah, my family. What a trip, *¿verdad?* They're the greatest thing I have going for me—not just personally, but professionally. As my mother has told me on many occasions, "Billy, *mira,* if you want to make it *como un* comedian, *lo único que tienes que hacer es hablar de tu familia en tu* own funny way."

Career-wise, *mis padres han sido bien* supportive. But my father wouldn't say, "*Te apoyamos*," as you would say in Spanish, or "We're backing you up," as you might say in English. Instead, *él le daba* his own Spanglish twist. *Él siempre me decía*, "Billy, your mother and I, *te estamos backeando* all the way."

He would have loved to see how much Spanish I am using on stage today. Of course, there are still some pretty significant pockets of Spanish resistance left out there. One time I opened my show by asking the audience, "Anybody here speak Spanish?" And, *se los lo juro por mi madre*, a guy in the front row looks at me and says, "No, thank God."

I was stunned. He really did catch me off guard. I'd never met anyone so defiantly monolingual. I couldn't believe it, *dándole las gracias a Dios* because he couldn't speak such a beautiful language. But in that moment, I pictured him getting to heaven, and the sign on the gate says: "*Se Habla Español*."

Perhaps the greatest *backeo* Papi ever provided was his insistence that my brothers and I learn Spanish. He was hardcore. My father would lock me and my brothers up in the car every year for the trip from New York to Florida, and the whole way we weren't allowed to speak anything but Spanish.

If you tried to speak to my father in English, he'd interrupt. "*No no no. Tiene que ser en español. ¡En español!*"

There were no exceptions. No matter what was going on.

"But Papi, there's a train coming! A train!"

"*¡En español!*"

"But a train!"

And you'd be freaking out at this point because your life was on the line and your Spanish wasn't kicking in. At which point I'd just desperately blurt out:

"*¡El Chooooooooo Choooooooooo!!!*"

The End, *por Ahora*

Well, *se acabó*. I'm done writing. You're done reading. And *de veras*, I hope *que* you enjoyed *el booko*. Truly, *ha sido un privilegio arrancar con este proyecto*. And if there's one lesson I want you to take away from *estas páginas*, it's this: English and Spanish have to team up. It's our only chance against Chinese.

Please come see a show sometime, and don't forget to say hi afterward. Feel free to send me your *Spanglishismos, que los necesitaré para el próximo librito*. And remember, *ésta no es una despedida*. Think of it more as an *hasta la* next time.

Porque because.